Disney, Leadership & You

House of the Mouse Ideas, Stories & Hope for the Leader in You

Written by

J. Jeff Kober

I0069278

Performance Journeys
TRAINING & DEVELOPMENT GROUP

Performance Journeys Publishing

© 2018 Performance Journeys Publishing

All rights reserved. No part of this book may be reproduced in any form—written, electronic, recording, or photocopying—without written permission of the publisher, except in the case of brief quotations or excerpts embodied in critical articles or reviews provided to the general public free of charge and for non-commercial purposes.

Although every precaution has been taken to verify the accuracy of the information contained herein, no responsibility is assumed for any errors or omissions, and no liability is assumed for damages that may result from the use of this information.

The views expressed in this book are those of the author alone. Neither Performance Journeys Publishing nor the author is affiliated with, authorized or endorsed by, or in any way officially connected with The Walt Disney Company, or any of its affiliates, or with any other business or governmental entity referenced within.

This book is an independent publication. Any references to copyrighted or trademarked intellectual property of The Walt Disney Company, or of other rights holders, are made strictly for editorial purposes, and no commercial claim upon that property is made by Performance Journeys Publishing or the author.

Performance Journeys publishes its books in a variety of print and electronic formats. Some content that appears in one format may not appear in another.

Editor: Leah Zanolla
Graphics: Justin Rucker

ISBN-13: 978-0999172605

Printed in the United States of America
Performance Journeys Publishing | www.PerformanceJourneys.com
Address queries to jeffkober@gmail.com

Dedicated to the most authentic, persevering, caring leader I know,

Kathy

How I love you, and admire you in every way.

Table of Contents

Forward by Danni Mikler

As I began to immerse myself in the many inside stories Jeff has compiled, I was transported to the early days of my own career. I considered the many lessons learned, and, most importantly, the Cast Members and Leaders who inspired me and made it possible to develop values and behaviors as a leader that would (hopefully!) impact the Guest Experience.

I am so honored that I was part of the story for four decades of my life through my role as a Disney Cast Member and Leader,.. and grateful for a career that included the privilege of piloting an authentic Paddle Wheel Steamship...providing Guest Tours of the Magic Kingdom.... and being part of the Epcot Opening team!

A defining moment in this journey occurred when I was offered the opportunity to manage Walt Disney World International Programs, with responsibility for the World Showcase Fellowship Program at Epcot...a role that supported Walt's plan for a diverse and inclusive Guest experience.

As this program grew significantly from 90 Students from 9 countries in 1982...I treasured the opportunity to train and mentor talented young leaders from over 67 countries who continue to be a resource for the global Disney organization and who can be found delivering consistently excellent service in Anaheim, Paris, Tokyo, Hong Kong, Shanghai, and throughout the Disney Cruise Line.... many in executive roles.

I had the good fortune to learn from Judi (Perry) Daley, Bob Mathieson, Lee Cockerell, Bill (Sully) Sullivan, Tom Nabbe, and George Kalogridis, and they all left their mark on my leadership values... always preserve the integrity of our product... with the core of our business being the Cast, and ultimately the "magic". Lessons learned include:

- Look for opportunities to go above and beyond in your service decisions.

- Model the behaviors that you want to instill in your team! Understand your Brand and make decisions that align.

- Be brave... even mistakes can turn into learning, if not magical moments!

- Be a great partner...try to say yes as often as you can!

- Celebrate diversity!

- Create "backstage magic"!

As to that last point, see the example of George Kalogridis, who some years before becoming president of the Walt Disney World Resort, served as head of Epcot during the Millennium celebration. He would have all of his leaders and the catering team on hand on New Year's Eve to serve the Cast as they headed out through Cast Services after the busiest night of the year! We served chili, sweet rolls, and hot chocolate (the expressions on their tired faces when they realized that their leaders were there to serve them at 4:00 am was just priceless!).

Jeff has introduced his readers to executives and leaders by sharing real examples of problem solving from the early days. He has also focused on the frontline Cast Members and entry level Leaders who create magic each day through their hard work and respect for Walt's vision and love for the brand. I treasure my friendship with Jeff and admire his gift for storytelling and his passion for "all things Disney"!

Welcome to Disney Leadership and the beginning of YOUR adventure! I'll end with my favorite words from Walt:

"Laughter is timeless, imagination has no age, and dreams are forever."

Danni Mikler

PREFACE
DEFINING DISNEY, LEADERSHIP & YOU

The title says it all. This book is about three things, and you are one of them!

Disney

This volume covers scores of leaders known and unknown within the Walt Disney Company. We study the qualities that make them great leaders, and our focus begins with Walt Disney himself. I never knew Walt personally. I was five when he passed away unexpectedly. But as a small child, I visited Disneyland and I came away with a curiosity, an interest, and an excitement that has not left me since.

One year as a child, my only Christmas presents were school socks and *The Art of Walt Disney* by Christopher Finch, an expensive coffee table book by 1970's standards. I begged for that book and I devoured it day in and day out. Later, I was among the first to purchase Bob Thomas' *Walt Disney, an American Original.* I now have full bookcases with hundreds of books, articles, and interviews focused solely on Disney. For nearly 5 decades, I have spent untold hours in the Disney archives and other libraries, trying to get a sense of the man and the impact he made. **What defines Walt Disney's legacy as a leader is that decades after his parting, people are still trying to understand, imitate, celebrate, and build upon the legacy he left behind.**

This book is not an attempt to put Walt Disney on a pedestal. Indeed, no leader is perfect, and that includes Walt Disney. Yet, there's something to be said for a man who drew so much loyalty out his staff and generations of viewers. **It is Walt**

Disney's continued leadership influence on his company, as well as on the world, that is so fascinating. As we examine Walt and the organization he founded, we hope to understand what works—and what doesn't work—when it comes to leading others.

That brings us to another note. No one idea in this book is universally represented in *every* facet of Disney—particularly in today's world. However, every concept demonstrates examples from the Disney organization of what it can and should look like. Again, like all companies, Disney is not perfect. Yet what is truly magical about Disney needs to be more universally held by all. I dedicate this book to those who are looking for a guide to becoming a better leader.

So, in short, I am excited to showcase, in my own way, the subject of Disney.

Leadership

I've also spent over 35 years in corporate training and development. From FedEx to Westin; from General Electric to Volkswagen; and from the City of New York to the U.S. Department of Education, I have taught principles and ideas for building a great organization. And from those experiences, what have I gleaned? **Great leaders fuel great organizations.** It's what is at the heart of the Chain Reaction of Excellence brought to light by my business partner, Mark David Jones, and I in our book, *Lead With Your Customer*. The chain is illustrated as follows:

LEADERSHIP EXCELLENCE — HIGHLY ENGAGED EMPLOYEES — HIGHLY SATISFIED CUSTOMERS — LOYALTY & LONG-TERM SUCCESS

If you want to be like Disney, a company that has had sustainable growth and long-term success for nearly an entire century, you must have highly satisfied customers. How do you achieve that? It takes a workforce that is enormously engaged. The domino that drives all of that is leadership excellence.

Great leaders in any organization are the catalysts for action, improvement, and excellence. Leaders who communicate a compelling vision, involve others, and effectively manage resources, create a fertile environment for achieving employee excellence--and thus the rest of the Chain Reaction of Excellence. Those qualities are the framework of this book. Indeed, we underscore many of those key points in bold throughout the book so that you can readily access them. We also summarize them in the last section.

You

The most important word in the title of this book is "You"! If the stories, ideas, and concepts from this book don't make a difference in your life, then what's it all for? For that reason we have framed this book for you with specific takeaways. At the end of each chapter, we ask questions for you to consider as a leader in moving your organization forward. We believe if you put into practice what we share in this book, it will serve you well in whatever path you pursue in this life.

For you, we offer inspiration. We want you to be invigorated by the messages herein. If you just believe, you will. These messages inspire me and have led me to think very differently about how I behave and associate with others—how I lead. Some of those personal tales, as painful as they were, I have shared as well.

Walt Disney noted: "Leadership implies a strong faith or belief in something." I hope I can fuel a belief that you can rise to a greater place, and that you can be the leader you envision for yourself. To that end, we dedicate our best efforts in the passages that follow, as well as in our workshops, seminars, and other resources.

Therefore, welcome to *Disney, Leadership & You*. As you continue through this volume, I offer the invitation of Timothy to Dumbo:

"Believe and Soar!"

SECTION
I

DEFINING LEADERSHIP

"My greatest reward, I think, is that I've been able to build this wonderful organization."

--Walt Disney

1

LEADERSHIP: THE MAGIC FORMULA
LEADERS CREATE THE MAGIC

Before we immerse ourselves into stories of Disney leadership, let's talk about leadership itself.

Think of a leader. It could be anyone. It could be someone famous. It could be someone you know personally or someone you've never met. It could be someone in the present or back in history. **When you think of a great leader, what quality can you define that makes them excel?** Is it one of these?

- Demonstrates courage

- Insightful and knowledgeable

- Works effectively with others

- Leads with a strong vision

- Persistent in overcoming challenges

- Acts with integrity

- Listens to others' needs

- Communicates well

- Walks the talk

- Proactively takes the lead

- Positive attitude no matter what

- Brings passion to what they do

We probably would all agree that great leaders hold many, if not all, of these qualities. Certainly as leaders, we can find our strengths and bring those talents to the table. What we do know is that to be a leader, you must exceed at the strengths you've been given. Remember, this book is about excellent leaders, not good leaders.

This book explores many of these talents, and considers how we can be of greater influence when we build on these strengths. Our objective is to see how you can be a leader, no matter what your role is in the organization.

Leaders Rise Up Throughout the Organization

Who is a leader? Many readers might assume that this book focuses on managers. Nothing could be further from the truth. Note that we didn't title this volume "Disney, Management & You". Quite the contrary. ***Every* employee can, and is expected to, exercise some type of leadership.** Go back to the previous list. *Every* employee can demonstrate these qualities. Each of these traits can be demonstrated among three groups of leadership: Positional, Spontaneous, and Personal. Let's look at each:

Positional Leadership. By virtue of someone holding a position of authority, they should also act and behave as a leader. Clearly Walt Disney fits here. His brother Roy O. Disney fits here. Anyone in management at Disney, from the CEO to a front line manager, should fit in this category. But let's consider the following: **Do you know someone who is a manager, but not necessarily a leader? If so, why?**

That is one of the things we will learn in this book. Some individuals lead in a particular way, but they fall short in other areas. Obviously, we would hope that all managers would act as leaders; however, that is not necessarily the case. As we highlight various leaders, we'll be honest about highlighting both strengths and weaknesses.

Another question to ask is: **Do you know someone who is not a manager, but who is definitely a leader? If so, why?**

The answer to this question stems from the two other types of leadership excellence—Spontaneous and Personal. Let's look at both.

Spontaneous Leadership. Individuals who take the lead and do great things in the hour of need are spontaneous leaders. Roy E. Disney, the son of Roy O. Disney, and the nephew of Walt, is a great example of spontaneous leadership. You would think such familial status would offer him an executive positional role in the family business; however, things didn't play out that way in the beginning. After both Walt and Roy O. had passed on, the company had become somewhat divided along family lines, with those who worked under Walt being dismissive of what Roy E. might bring to the table. While Roy was involved with making films for the company—even holding a seat on the board—he held little strategic control. To guard off a hostile takeover that would dismantle the company and sell off its assets, he finally had to step away from the board and organize a consortium of white knight investors to step into the middle of it. He led in a time of crisis. Interesting that he stepped away from any degree of control to focus on how he could influence from the outside.

In doing this, he brought Michael Eisner and Frank Wells into the company. This spontaneous leadership on Roy E. Disney's part led to a new renaissance of enormous growth for the company. Two decades later, he repeated the same process, exercising again spontaneous leadership after Frank Wells' death when Eisner's role in Disney had turned the company in a negative direction. Again, Roy E. Disney stepped away from the board of directors to lead a "Save Disney" campaign to have Michael Eisner removed from the company. That ousting led Bob Iger into the role of CEO.

Spontaneous crisis leadership like that of Roy E. Disney might mean taking the lead by being the first to:

- Initiate action
- Take ownership of any circumstance that might come up
- Accomplish the work
- Hang in there when others give up
- Defend that which must be defended
- Get on board to change when needed

There are other individuals in the history of the Walt Disney Company who provided spontaneous leadership—many of whom were not in the public eye, like Joe Fowler and Michael M. Grilikhes. We'll study their experiences as well.

Do you know of someone who, in the hour of need in your organization, stepped up to the plate and helped save the day? What did they do that made them spontaneous leaders?

Personal Leadership. The third, and incredibly important, type of leadership is Personal Leadership. Every employee should practice personal leadership. This means we should accept responsibility and act consistently to be our best each and every day. We should do the very best in the role we have. It can look like any of the following:

- Taking pride and ownership in the work we are assigned to do and that others expect of us.
- Taking on extra loads, even when it's not convenient.
- Remembering someone's anniversary or birthday, when others have forgotten.
- Focusing on getting work done well and on time.
- Being anticipatory in your work.
- Not participating in rumors or gossip.
- Being available when others have gone home early.

People usually dismiss the role a front-line worker can play in an organization. The most dismissed of these are personal assistants or secretaries. Not so at Disney. Walt's first official secretary was Lillian Bounds. She would later marry Walt and be more influential than any, even to the naming of Walt's greatest creation, Mickey Mouse.

Later, it was another of Walt's secretaries, Tommie Blount Wilck, who suggested Julie Andrews play the role of Mary Poppins. He was so trusting of her advice that Walt would refer to Tommie as his "secretary of the exterior."

Hazel George, the studio nurse, also had an influence on Walt. He would often retreat to her office next door to get heat treatments for ongoing pain that had its origins from a polo accident. They would refer to the office as "The Laughing Place", a retreat for Br'er Rabbit in *Song of the South*. There, at the end of the studio workday, he found someone he could confide in.

On one occasion, Walt was in a reflective mood and told Hazel: "You know, I finally found out who I am."

"Who are you?" Hazel asked.

"I'm the last of the benevolent monarchs."

She thought about it and replied: "That's good. Now I know what I am."

"What's that?"

"The last of the court jesters."

As court jester, she moved outside the boundaries of any clinical nurse. She often read movie scripts, and would offer suggestions. When an album came out based on the film *Pollyanna*, she wrote alternate lyrics to the song "The Glad Game" under the name of Gil George. When Walt asked her if she would like to contribute to the building of Disneyland, she not only agreed, but then went about forming an organization of studio workers, called the

Backers and the Boosters. The effort made Roy O. Disney more open to his brother's efforts to build the park.

The last day he ever spent at the studio, Walt stopped to see Hazel. "Well, here we are in the 'Laughing Place,'" he said, studying her reaction to his gaunt appearance from cancer.

"There's something I want to tell you–", he said, but the words wouldn't come. Instead, they embraced each other, weeping.

Walt would pass away a few days later.

Do you know of someone who is a personal leader? What qualities do they exhibit? What are some examples of how they have been a leader?

Leadership On All Fronts. Returning again to Roy E. Disney, he not only played a spontaneous role that led to a change of leadership at the top, but eventually went on to play a positional role, heading the return and renaissance of Disney animation. Roy made possible such classics as *The Little Mermaid, Beauty & The Beast, Aladdin,* and *The Lion King.* He didn't draw, or even direct, them, but he became the leading influence that made them possible. It's an example of how you can lead on all three fronts.

What's the message here? **There are three types of leaders: positional, spontaneous, and personal.** The presence of all three leadership types together, and even their convergence, is what constitutes leadership excellence. That kind of overlap creates a culture and environment for excellence that you can't achieve otherwise.

Leaders Exercise Influence, Not Control

The brilliance of Disney and any great organization is when leadership happens on all three levels. In order for this to happen, there must be a culture—a place—where everyone can be a leader. Not in some "too many chefs in the kitchen" mentality, but in a place where everyone exercises influence.

In *Seven Habits of Highly Effective People*, Stephen R. Covey speaks of three overlaying circles in one's life:

- Circle of Control
- Circle of Influence, but No Control
- Circle of No Control and No Influence

Those circles, which move from the center outward, are used by Dr. Covey to describe how one should manage his or her time. The notion here is to pay attention to those things you can control and/or influence, as opposed to those things you cannot. That model is useful, but it has another use as well, particularly in our role as leaders. Let's describe each in greater detail.

Circle of Control. In the center are those things we can control. We may not be in charge of much, but whatever it is we control, that inner circle defines it. We may be responsible for budgets, labor, or policies. In an organization, those with no positional authority have a small circle. Those who are managers have a much larger circle. Those at the executive level wield the largest circle of control.

Circle of Influence, but no Control. The next circle defines what we cannot control, but can influence. There are many things we can influence, even though the ability to make the decision is not ours.

Circle of No Control or Influence. The third circle describes those things we can neither control nor influence. An example of this might be the weather or a war somewhere on the other side of the globe. We might have some control over our response to those events, but we have neither control nor influence to do anything about them.

Where do great leaders best spend their time? Clearly, we should be responsible for that which is in our control, the smallest of all circles. But where many fail is in their inability to see potential in focusing on that which they can influence, even if they have no control. That is the most powerful opportunity.

There are three important notions that emerge from this model:

1. Many believe that to be a stronger leader, they must gain more control. They believe if they were just in a "bigger position," if they could just "run things around here," or if they could simply "be in charge," they would be a greater leader. That paradigm, however, is incorrect. **You may manage more people, but that will not necessarily make you a greater leader.**

2. Those who have a smaller circle of control simply "give up" by making statements like, "there's nothing I can do, I'm not in charge." That too is an erroneous mindset. **There is much that leaders can do to influence, even when they are not the one in charge.**

3. The correct notion is that people do not become greater leaders because they were the one in charge, or because they had a greater circle of control. **Great leaders exist because they have established a larger circle of influence.**

Leaders Focus on Results & Relationships

In the following model, we want to introduce two key attributes that make up a leader. They form the outline of this book.
This chart represents two important factors in leadership. You'll see that the horizontal axis of this grid is about results. It's about *what* we produce or do. The vertical axis is about relationships. This axis is about *how* we do what we do. Let's walk through this matrix:

+

↑

QUADRANT B   **QUADRANT A**

RELATIONSHIPS

QUADRANT D   **QUADRANT C**

- ——————————————→ +

RESULTS

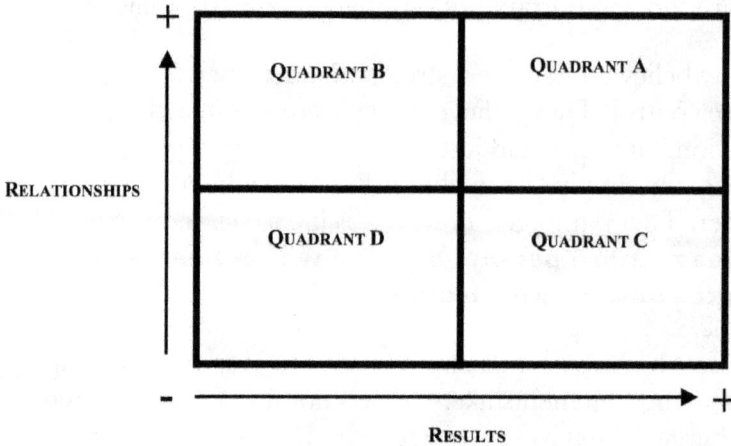

This matrix is divided into four quadrants. It illustrates where leaders best succeed, which is from focusing on attaining results by effectively working with others. As we review the first three, think about those individuals you associate with and where they might fall. Also, consider your own strengths and weaknesses and where you fall on this grid.

Quadrant D: Hopefully no one in an organization falls into this category. The reality is though, there's always one. In this category, individuals not only fail to perform, but they spend their time frustrating those around them. They become an island unto themselves. If the organization is worth its weight, they should be concerned with the future of any who fall in this box.

Quadrant C: In this quadrant, managers measure accomplishments through deadlines, budgets, and projects, but they may be burning bridges in other's paths as they master those achievements. Employees become easily frustrated with them, and resent how they are treated. Others in the organization think they have no voice in what is going on. They feel their own contribution is unacknowledged, and as a result, they withdraw their own passion and detach themselves from all that is toxic.

Quadrant B: The reverse of this is also true. One can be a great team player and get along with others. They can be the life of the office, but in terms of getting work done, they fail to perform to what is required of them. Goals end up being unaccomplished or others complete them in their stead.

Quadrant A: Where real leaders emerge is in Quadrant A. These leaders are not only good at getting results but work effectively with others as well. **Great leadership is about not only *what* you do, but also *how* you do it.**

As a reminder, this is a book on leadership excellence. It's not just about being in Quadrant A. It's about being the best of the best—being in the top right hand corner of that quadrant. It takes excellent leaders—not *good* leaders—to engage others in achieving results.

These two qualities are so important that we have framed this book into two major sections: Attaining Results and Building Relationships. Let's look at an example of two individuals and where they fall on this spectrum.

Two Leaders: Walt Disney and Louis B. Mayer

For many years, Disney's Hollywood Studios was called Disney-MGM Studios. To that end, the entrance arch featured both Mickey Mouse and Leo the Lion. When the park was first built, Michael Eisner thought that the Disney name would be insufficient to attract tourists who wanted to visit an authentic, working studio. Eisner wanted to link it up with a bigger name. In the 1930s and 1940s, the time period represented by the park's Hollywood & Sunset Boulevards, there were seven major motion picture studios. The biggest of them was the infamous MGM (Metro Goldwyn Mayer) Studios headed by Louis B. Mayer. From the end of the silent film era through World War II, MGM was known as having "more stars than there are in heaven", a reference to the large number of famous movie stars under contract with the company. Disney gained the rights to use the MGM name for a bargain price during the development of the new park in the 1980s.

At the other end of the spectrum from MGM back in the 30s and 40s, **Disney was "the little studio that could".** It ranked as number seven, even after Walt Disney passed away. A study of Disney and Mayer's approaches as studio heads offers important insights into what makes a successful positional leader.

Walt Disney. Most don't recall the name Donnie Dunagan. At age 18, he enlisted in the Marine Corps, becoming the Marines' youngest-ever drill instructor. He would serve three tours in Vietnam, and in the end, received a Bronze Star and the Purple Heart. But his earliest accomplishment was being the voice of Bambi. To Donnie, Walt made an indelible impression on him. After not only working for Disney, but also serving years on the battlefield, Donnie drew the following conclusion:

> Mr. Disney was not a pompous executive aristocratic leader. He had his sleeves rolled up. He participated in everything. And when he would come around to an art activity or to a sound activity, people were eager to see him. The employees were eager to see him. The artists were eager to see him. In other studios, when the boss was coming around, people would go, oh gosh, here comes the boss, watch out...watch out. Hide that. Don't ask him. Be quiet. Not with Mr. Disney. Everybody wanted him around, because he participated. And he had great ideas, and they would listen to him, in a respectful way, and not like the boss.

Here is how Walt's daughter, Diane Disney Miller, summed up her father:

> Walt was unquestionably one of the most demanding bosses an employee could ever have. He didn't hesitate to cut down an employee with a harsh word, or even a public tirade. He was uncompromising in his desire for quality, and he held his staff to the same high standards as he did himself. What's more, he never thought

money was the reason to do good work, and he had difficulty understanding others whose main motivation was cash.

And though more than one staffer left the Disney Studio unhappily, many others stayed with Walt for years—some for up to 5 or 6 decades. Thirty years after his death, a number of former employees still welled up with tears when they talked about his passing. This is hardly the mark of a "mean boss."

Louis B. Mayer. In contrast, Louis B. Mayer, studio head at MGM Studios, said, "My philosophy is quite simple. I hire the best people. Then I give them plenty of freedom to do their best. And if I don't like their best work, I fire them."

This philosophy is known as "Bring me a rock." It's a frequently played-out tactic among demanding managers. If managers like the rock (presentation, idea, whatever), then everything is great. But if they don't like it, you're expected to bring a new "rock" in a short time frame. Little, if any, criteria, feedback, or understanding is provided. You're simply expected to bring the right rock. And if you don't deliver, you're often terminated. "Give me more musicals." "Put Garland in a better picture." MGM Studios survived because it kept bringing more "rocks" to the theater.

That philosophy did pay off in many ways. Some of the most beloved movies were created through this studio system, to include *The Wizard of Oz, Singin' in the Rain,* and *Gone with the Wind.* At one time, Mayer was the richest man in the world, and many, like Robert Taylor and Greer Garson, viewed him like a father figure. Still others, like Elizabeth Taylor, described him as a monster. Samuel Goldwyn stated: "The only reason so many people attended his funeral was they wanted to make sure he was dead."

In Mindy Johnson's terrific in-depth look at the women of Disney's animation studio, *Ink & Paint,* she notes a story where the two men, Walt Disney and Louis B. Mayer, met. Blanche Sewell, a film editor, arranged for a screening of some of Walt's shorts at MGM. This was back before *Snow White*. Walt apologetically mentioned that the shorts were "rather crudely done…" Blanche cut him short. 'Don't apologize, Walt. I wouldn't have called them in here if I didn't think your stuff was great!"

The projectionist ran a Mickey Mouse reel, followed by *Springtime*, a Silly Symphony short for several MGM directors. Several were present, including directors George Hill and Victor Fleming, and Frances Marion, a screenwriter who was so "lost in dreams" that she dragged Mr. Mayer down to see the shorts himself. Stopping the film before its end, Mayer shouted "Ridiculous! Women and men dance together. Boys and girls dance together…But flowers! Bah!" While viewing the Mickey Mouse short, Mayer shouted, "Stop that film! Stop it at once! Every woman is scared of a mouse, admit it…And here you think they're going to laugh at a mouse on the screen that's ten feet high!"

Laughed is what audiences did. They also clapped and teared up, especially when *Snow White and the Seven Dwarfs* came into the theaters. It was that film's worldwide success that led MGM to green-light the *Wizard of Oz* for production. Victor Fleming, who saw those shorts that day, inevitably directed it. And Blanche Sewell became the lead editor for the film.

Leaders Leave a Legacy

In short, one studio head treated his employees and others as commodities. Another treated his employees as vital assets to be nurtured and developed.

Both Walt Disney and Louis B. Mayer were demanding. They held high expectations of their employees and were very direct in their approach. Both created unforgettable cinematic experiences for the public. But only one left a legacy with his employees, and in the end, that made all the difference in the world. MGM has been bought, sold, and put into bankruptcy several times over. It has been largely dismantled to the point that it cannot even be ranked as being in last place.

Meanwhile, the Walt Disney Company has risen to be the number one studio in the world. **Walt's vision, his sacrifices, and his persistence in life have fueled the company decades after he departed from this life.** It is Walt Disney's leadership and example that continue to take the company to new heights even today.

Leadership & You

This writings in this chapter have outlined examples of leadership and Disney. Now, it's about leadership and you. At the end of every chapter, we'll direct that magic mirror toward you, allowing you to consider more deeply your own leadership efforts. Ask yourself:

- How do I nurture and develop my employees?

- Is one type of leadership more important to me than others? Are all equal?

- What happens when organizations focus only on positional leadership, but fail to practice personal and spontaneous leadership?

- What are areas of responsibility I have control over? How am I accountable for the success of those areas of responsibility? Can I effectively control others when I exercise little influence?

- What are areas I have no control over, but do have influence over? How can I better influence the outcomes of issues that impact me, but I have no final say in?

- What are areas I have neither control nor influence over? How can I put aside my concern and attention around those areas in which I do not have control or influence?

- What are the qualities of a great leader?

- Do I spend more time increasing my area of control by being the one in charge? Will these things ultimately make me a better leader?

- How can I increase my influence with others through my own courage, vision and performance?

- How do others know of my concern and interest in them as individuals?

- If a child observed me at work, how would he summarize my ability to lead others?

- How can I expect the best in others, without being demanding and unreasonable?

- What kind of legacy do I want to leave after it's all over? How do I want to be remembered?

SECTION
II

LEADERS ATTAIN RESULTS

"You don't know what you can do until you try."

"The imagining was much easier to do than the doing."

"People often ask me if I know the secret of success...and could tell others how to make their dreams come true. My answer is you do it by working."

--Walt Disney

2

THERE'S A
GREAT BIG BEAUTIFUL TOMORROW
LEADERS STAY THE VISION

Step onto Main Street, U.S.A. in any of the Magic Kingdom parks around the globe and you feel a spirit of optimism. There's a spring in your step and a feeling that all is right with the world. Of course, this isn't reality—it is in no way a faithful reproduction of any one city in the country, not even Walt's childhood home of Marceline, Missouri. However, it does provide us a glimpse of how Walt saw the world before him and how a growing America saw the new twentieth century.

Walt depicted the best of the twentieth century in a show he prepared for the New York World's Fair, entitled *The Carousel of Progress*. The show was Walt's own idea. Each act represented a time in history. Threaded throughout the show was the Sherman Brothers' anthem, "There's a Great Big Beautiful Tomorrow":

> *There's a great, big beautiful tomorrow*
> *Shining at the end of every day*
> *There's a great, big, beautiful tomorrow*
> *And tomorrow's just a dream away*
>
> *Man has a dream and that's the start*
> *He follows his dream with mind and heart*
> *And when it becomes a reality*
> *It's a dream come true for you and me*
>
> *So there's a great, big beautiful tomorrow*
> *Shining at the end of every day*

There's a great, big, beautiful tomorrow
Just a dream away

Perhaps it's simplistic in its message, but millions enjoyed it when it first played in New York. Additionally, tens of millions more have seen it since at both Disneyland and Walt Disney World. People want to believe in a better tomorrow. Leaders believe there is a better tomorrow and despite the challenges, are persistent in making dreams become a reality.

Walt Disney's Road to Failure
LEADERS TRIUMPH BEYOND THEIR FAILURES

When you think of success, it's easy to think of Walt Disney. Surely he was successful. He created more than 81 feature films and hundreds of shorts. He earned more than 950 honors, including 32 Academy Awards from 59 nominations. He founded the California Institute of the Arts, and he built Disneyland. Yet by the time that park opened in 1955, Walt had been through many less than successful ventures. Most people see the cotton-candied side of Walt's success, but few really have contemplated the struggles and painful difficulties that brought him to this point. **One doesn't become defined as optimistic in the absence of fear.** Rather, it is often honed through failure. And, yet, from hard times came important lessons and events, which would serve Walt Disney throughout his life. Walt experienced painful, difficult moments, but out of them, he grew, and in many ways, triumphed. For comparative purposes, let's look at several challenging milestones.

Family Entertainment from a Dysfunctional Family
Walt's brothers were so frustrated about their relationship with their dad that, one by one, they all ran away from home early in their lives. First it was brothers Herb and Ray over a dispute about money they had earned. Later it would be Roy, who, at 19, believed he was treated like a little boy by his father's domineering attitude. Eager to move on himself, Walt lied about his age so he could be an ambulance driver during World War I.

Despite the dysfunctional relationships he and his family experienced, Walt Disney became the leader and the voice of family entertainment. Of Disneyland, he would comment how badly he wanted a place where children and parents could enjoy time together. Millions of families continue to come together because of entertainment created by Walt Disney and the legacy he left behind. And despite differences with their father, Walt, along with his brother Roy, did their best to honor and respect their parents throughout their lives.

Bankruptcy in Kansas City. Barely into his twenties, Walt's first enterprise fell into bankruptcy after the failure of a cartoon series in Kansas City. He headed to Los Angeles with $40 in cash, and an imitation-leather suitcase containing only a shirt, two pairs of undershorts, two pairs of socks, and some drawing materials. Feeling that others did animation better, his goal was to be an actor in Hollywood. This goal was never realized and he was quickly penniless. Visiting his brother Roy in the hospital, who was recuperating from tuberculosis, he borrowed $5 to pay his Uncle Robert for room and board.

The upside was that he and Roy realized there was no animation business headquartered in California. They set up their own animation studio on October 16, 1923. The rest is history. Over time, the Disney brothers became the most successful team in Hollywood, largely because they depended on the strengths of each other.

Anything but Lucky. One of Walt's first animated successes was Oswald the Lucky Rabbit. Under the distributorship of Universal, he created and sold a series of silent film cartoons. But those shorts became increasingly expensive for the return he was receiving. On a trip to New York to re-negotiate the agreement, Walt not only learned that he legally had no ownership of the character, but that most of the artists who worked for him had committed themselves to working for the distributor instead. Essentially, Walt's entire organization was taken from him. Still, in a memo from New York to his brother Roy, he wrote, "Don't worry. I really do feel that everything will turn out all right.

Anyways I believe that whatever does happen is FOR THE BEST."

Then, on a train ride back from that fateful meeting in New York, Walt created a new character. He named him Mortimer Mouse. Wisely, Walt listened to the counsel of his wife when she suggested that Mickey might be more suitable. So Mickey it was!

But having the right name does not a successful cartoon make. Walt's first attempts to build a Mickey Mouse short were met with little interest. Walt knew he needed something that would make Mickey stand out. Warner Brother's premiere of the first major talking picture, *The Jazz Singer*, was a sign that Walt needed to create the first talking cartoon. Out of his uncle's garage came *Steamboat Willie*. And the rest is history.

Walt would say, "It all began with a mouse." In truth, the little personality that would serve as the symbol of the entire company began as a humble, down and out struggle.

"A Heck of a Breakdown." In the early 1930s, Walt suffered what he called "a heck of a breakdown." He was anxious about the ability of cartoon shorts to deliver a serious profit. Beyond being irritable with his employees, the breakdown included many sleepless nights. There were story sessions where he was completely unfocused and unable to contribute. He would even plunge into crying spells at a moment's notice. At the urging of others, he and his wife planned a second honeymoon on a long-anticipated voyage down the Mississippi River. Unfortunately, when they arrived at the St. Louis waterfront, they found out that the Great Depression had wiped out the passenger trade. They had to go elsewhere to vacation.

Ironically, days before Disneyland opened in 1955, Lillian and Walt would celebrate their anniversary by taking their invited friends on the first trip down the Rivers of America on the newly built Mark Twain Steamboat. One wonders if Walt's disappointing second honeymoon wasn't the event that inspired the creation of this paddle wheeler years later.

Still, returning from that second honeymoon, Walt was refreshed and ready to start on something really ambitious: the development of a full-length animated feature we would come to know as *Snow White and the Seven Dwarfs*. It would be a triumphant success.

A Parent's Death. From the extraordinary success of *Snow White and the Seven Dwarfs*, Walt and Roy built a home for their aging parents in California. Having them close by would allow the brothers to care for their parents while juggling busy schedules. Unfortunately, poor construction by contractors and subsequent attempts at repairing it by studio workmen ended in their mother dying one morning from carbon monoxide poisoning. Walt and Roy were devastated by their mother's death.

Nothing could fix or replace losing their mother in such a tragic accident. However, while there may be little, if any, connection, it is interesting to note that in Walt's later years, he conceptualized a community where many of the challenges of urban life would be resolved. That was the original concept of E.P.C.O.T., where concepts in architecture, transportation, and infrastructure would serve to provide a better tomorrow, today.

"The Crime of the Century." Walt and Lillian raised two daughters in the wake of what was noted as "The Crime of the Century". This was in reference to the abduction and murder of Charles Lindbergh's 20-month-old son in 1932. With Walt being not only a celebrity, but also a prominent individual in terms of family entertainment, they became concerned about having their own children be seen in the public eye. They took many steps to protect their children, right down to reinforcing the window screens on their Los Feliz home.

Mindful of protecting their daughters, Walt and Lilly spent many nights at home. They weren't Hollywood socialites. They cherished their daughters, who, in return, deeply loved their parents. Walt himself would accompany his children on daddy-daughter trips, many of which led him to early thoughts about building an amusement park enterprise. That idea for a place that families could enjoy together would become Disneyland.

Strike! Just prior to World War II, Walt experienced an acrimonious strike by his animators. The experience severed him from artists with whom he had thought he was close. To settle the strike, his brother sent him away to South America on a goodwill tour for the U.S.

From this goodwill tour came the films *Saludos Amigos* and *The Three Caballeros*. More importantly, it may be that Walt's 'South American Sabbatical' gave him time to think about his organization and how he wanted to be a leader. Walt learned the importance of teamwork. He said: "Whatever we accomplish is due to the combined effort. The organization must be with you or you don't get it done."

The New Spirit. On the morning following December 7, 1941, the United States Army took over the Walt Disney Studios as a repair shop for tanks and artillery. Walt's artists went to war. Worldwide markets were closed to film distribution. Walt himself had to have a government ID to get on his own property. While working on government projects, bookkeepers would question all expenditures.

On one project for the U.S. Treasury Department, Walt created a film starring Donald Duck called *The New Spirit*. The film did much to inspire Americans to pay their taxes, something not commonly done back then. Those monies helped win the war. That, and many other projects Walt took on at that time, helped to support the war effort during those years.

"The Lost Years." After World War II, the company had more than $4 million in debts, and business was very slow in the war's aftermath. The company was distributing films in Europe but they had difficulty getting monies to come back to the Studios in the United States. Described by Roy O. Disney as "the lost years," he told Walt after a heated exchange one night: "Look, you're letting this place drive you to the nuthouse. That's one place I'm not going with you!" Still, Walt struggled to deal with the stress he was facing.

With monies held in Europe, they began producing some of their first feature films overseas. This endeavor prompted Walt to diversify his product beyond animation. Ultimately, the success of the Walt Disney Studios would not have happened if he had only produced animation features.

It was also during this time that Walt took up Roy's suggestion to get a hobby. He took up an interest in trains. That railroad interest fueled the fire for building a theme park—one with a train running around it.

Needing Money. Walt needed to find the money to build Disneyland. The banks were slow to financially back him up, weary of the thought of putting so much money into a carnival. One idea Walt had was to enter the business of television by having ABC sponsor his park in exchange for him creating TV shows. At that time, the major Hollywood studios put pressure on each other not to support television production, as it would ruin the movie business. The studios feared that people would stop going to the movies and just stay home watching the tube.

Walt broke ranks and went with television anyway. From this leap of faith, we have classics like *The Mickey Mouse Club* and *Disneyland*, which served to promote the park he was building. Moreover, Walt gained the financing to open Disneyland.

"Black Sunday." On July 17, 1955, Walt Disney dedicated Disneyland before a television audience of millions. Meanwhile, forged tickets were bringing thousands of people into the park without his knowledge. The newly poured asphalt melted, causing the heels of women's shoes to get stuck, and a plumbers' strike kept drinking fountains from being installed in time. Critics blasted it as "Black Sunday."

Walt resisted allowing the park to become poorly cared for. He held the park to high standards of customer service, as well as great attention to detail. The result was that Disneyland became a phenomenal success, spawning other parks, and creating a critical component of the Walt Disney Company.

By the time folks walked onto Main Street, U.S.A. on the Black Sunday of 1955, so much had gone on in the decades before. Main Street had been paved with not just hopes and dreams, but also tears and fears. But through it all, Walt learned that the power of making dreams come true required being positive and persistent, even in the face of difficulty.

Of this, Walt said:

"To some people, I am kind of a Merlin who takes lots of crazy chances, but rarely makes mistakes. I've made some bad ones, but, fortunately, the successes have come along fast enough to cover up the mistakes. **When you go to bat as many times as I do, you're bound to get a good average."**

Alan Coats, son of Imagineer Claude Coats, noted: "Walt Disney had a larger view of the future than most people. Even more important, Walt knew how to make the future happen."

The perspective that leaders could press forward in their vision, despite the obstacles, was passed on to new generations. Walt Disney would never see the opening of Walt Disney World and other projects he imagined, but he inspired a team of people who would make that happen even in his absence. Here are other examples of that determination:

A Wave of Possibilities
LEADERS ALLOW THE VISION TO UNFOLD

Dick Nunis began work for the company at the time Disneyland opened, and in the subsequent years, was promoted to executive vice president by the time Walt Disney World opened in 1971. His vision for the "Vacation Kingdom of the World" was for it to compete against its biggest competitor—Florida beaches and the oceans they bordered. Dick loved to surf, and he felt that Disney needed waves big enough to surf on. So tenacious was he at petitioning this to happen with senior management, and especially Roy O. Disney, that he eventually received $400,000 to build a wave machine on the Seven Seas Lagoon. The result was ocean-like waves that washed upon the white sandy beaches adjacent to Disney's Polynesian Resort.

The wave machine was installed before the Seven Seas Lagoon was completely filled with water, and by the summer of 1971, months before the property opened, the machine did create waves. Unfortunately, it didn't last long. Within months, it began breaking down not long after it started up each day. Those in water transportation complained that it was difficult to maneuver in and out with the waves. Worse, when the machine was cranking out waves, it began to erode the beaches that had been put in place. In time, the machine was declared dead.

But that didn't end Dick's interest in creating a wave machine for Walt Disney World. A few years later, River Country opened up as America's first water park. Designed initially to really serve the resort Guests staying in and around the Magic Kingdom, the popularity of the "old-fashioned swimming hole" led Dick to petition for an even bigger water park. And since other water parks like Wet 'n Wild had introduced wave pools, Dick thought Disney could create a water park so big that the wave pool could have 'surf-style waves.'

Years had passed since the failed attempt at creating ocean currents. By then, the technology had changed, but the solution to creating consistent waves really came from an old idea—flushing the toilet. With water filling a set of individual chambers along a themed back wall, all that would be needed would be to flush the water into the 2.7 million gallon wave pool. Dick knew this time he had a winner as he watched the wave pool be tested for the first time. So strong were the waves that they broke through the beach and flowed over into Castaway Creek.

In June 1989, Disney's Typhoon Lagoon was inaugurated with Dick Nunis surfing the first wave. It remains the most popular water park in the world. The water park was so popular that a sister park, Blizzard Beach, opened afterwards with its own wave pool. This winter-themed water park boasted even more slides than Typhoon Lagoon, becoming another testament to Dick Nunis' tenacity to create a place for people to come play in the water.

What began as a competitor to Walt Disney World—the beach and ocean—is now Disney's domain as well, with a fleet of award-winning cruise ships. Disney even has its own private island surrounded by the ocean. **Perhaps Walt Disney could never imagine a cruise line in his name. But Walt did live a life and provide a vision that inspired others to do so decades later.** It is his life that inspired others to take dreams to a new level.

That same tenacity is part of the Walt Disney Company today. Here are two examples:

Authentically Disney, Distinctly Chinese: Shanghai Disneyland
LEADERS HAVE A LONG-TERM VIEW

The Chinese expression *"Three feet of ice is not formed in a single day"* certainly holds true for Shanghai Disneyland. Since Disneyland opened over six decades ago, the folks at Disney have learned a few lessons. The Japanese totally embraced the first international park when it opened Tokyo Disneyland. But when Disney opened Disneyland Paris in a former sugar beet field outside Paris in 1992, the company was roundly criticized for being culturally insensitive to its European Guests. Hong Kong Disneyland opened modestly, and has struggled to compete with a local competitor, even with newer additions.

In 2016, Shanghai Disneyland premiered to a new massive population of potential visitors. It is an enormous undertaking that involves a Magic Kingdom-style park, two resort hotels, a shopping district, and a lakefront park. Still, this is not just about replicating a Magic Kingdom in China. It's about creating China's Magic Kingdom. It has to be something the Chinese people embrace and make their own. Certainly there is a potential market to make that happen. Some 330 million of China's 1.3 billion people live within a three-hour drive or train ride from Shanghai, an enormous metropolis of 24 million. This should give the resort a leg up for being successful.

But that success is only sustained if people enjoy the experience so much that they return again and again to visit, and they promote visiting the park to others around them. The view "build it and they will come" is a poor approach to what is a $5.5 billion dollar investment, Disney's most expensive theme park destination to date. Disney must win the hearts of its Guests—Guests who for the most part have never entered a Disney park before. And that must take time—and patience.

When Bob Iger stepped on stage in 2016 to open Shanghai Disneyland Resort, he stated, "Anything is possible for those who believe." He also said, "If someone said in 1999, 'Well, you'll eventually have a resort here, but it won't be until 2016', most people would have said 'Don't spend any time on this; it's too long.' Yet we stayed at it." **Like Walt Disney's legacy has shown, dreams are not only big, but they take many years to bring to fruition.**

Floating Ideas on Pandora
LEADERS MOVE FORWARD NOT KNOWING

Many who have viewed the film *Avatar* were inspired by the amazing worlds dreamed up by James Cameron. They took celluloid form in a blockbuster film that was seen the world over. But here's the catch: None of those forests and animals were real—they were all computer graphics. No physical sets of Pandora were created for the film. Actors had to appear before green screens and the world was drawn around them in post-production. Viewers were immersed in a totally imaginary world. Disney Imagineer Joe Rohde led the effort to build the Adventurer's Club, Disney's Animal Kingdom, and Aulani, a Disney Resort & Spa. When he was tasked to physically build the world of Pandora in Disney's Animal Kingdom, he had a tall order ahead of him. So tall that floating islands would have to appear as if they were hanging in mid-air, without any appearance of having structural support. And if that were not enough—the mountains would need to have water flowing down from them 24 hours a day. Finally, at night it would all have to glow as though it were one giant bioluminescent forest. On Pandora's opening day, Bob Iger noted: "At Disney we have a 'how did they do that' standard...I can't think of a better example of that than what we're standing in front of right now." Cameron responded: "I never thought I'd see the day when the Pandora I imagined could be made physically real."

After years of designing and building, that dream is finally a reality. But it didn't come without gaining the confidence to build on the dream over time. That confidence came from hard, persistent work on previous projects. On an episode of the *Season Pass* podcast, Joe Rohde spoke about the daunting challenge of Imagineering. Disney's Animal Kingdom originally:

> There was a moment after we had received capital authorization to build the park, and I had finally relocated to Florida, and I'm walking around on this giant site—which is already cleared—they were starting to build...I was terrified—just terrified. Terrified. Terrified. Because I'm thinking, "What the heck! What do I know? What do I know? I don't know. I thought it was a good idea. I don't know. I don't know!"

> And you don't know for a long time and then finally, like a year and a half later, when you're finally seeing it coming up, then I could go, "Okay, this is pretty cool. I think it's

going to be cool. I think it's going to be real cool." But for the longest time, it's just like…because… you get whipped up in the enthusiasm for your project. You got to sell it. You got to do it. You got to love your project. But then once you're building it, and it's such a huge site…No one has ever done it before and it's totally different, and you think, "What the heck!" So it was really scary for yeah…six months for sure…For sure. I mean really stomach achy…and like not sleeping. Did I make a horrible mistake? But I don't think so. I really think it's a lovely place and people seem to really love it…

…I think if you are going to do something that has never been done before, then you don't get to know whether it's going to work or not. That's part of what you have to live with. If it hadn't been done before, then don't lie about it. You don't know if it's going to work. You're going to try it. You're going to do your best. Use your best thinking—and your best behaviour—and your best design. But you don't know. It's the future, right? You don't know. **But you have to have the courage to at least try it, or else we'd all be sitting on a tree branch in Africa!**

"Who's Afraid of the Big Bad Wolf?"
LEADERS OPEN NEW DOORS IN TOUGH TIMES

Having a dream and making it a reality are two different themes. And what separates the two is usually a crucible of difficult challenges. **What gets one across that bridge between the dream and reality is optimism. It is having a positive attitude.**

Walt's brother, Roy O. Disney, once spoke of the Great Depression:

> When the banks were closed in 1933, of course I was frantic—what are we gonna do for money? So I was stewing and worrying and Walt was impatient with me.

He [Walt] said, "Quit worrying about it. People aren't going to stop living just because the banks are closed. What the hell, we'll make potatoes the medium of exchange. We'll pay everybody in potatoes."

"Who's Afraid of the Big Bad Wolf" was a popular tune by Frank Churchill (who later wrote the songs for *Snow White and the Seven Dwarfs*) and was tied to Disney's *Silly Symphony* success, *The Three Little Pigs*. It came at a time when the country was embroiled in a deep depression. It also speaks of working through one's fears and difficulties through action and effort. Walt Disney noted the following:

"People sort of live in the dark about things. A lot of young people think the future is closed to them, that everything has been done. This is not so. There are still plenty of avenues to be explored...**For youngsters of today, I say believe in the future, the world is getting better, there is still plenty of opportunity."**

Leaders build on the power of dreaming. And they build on the power of persistence. It's healthy to reflect on what has been, how much better things are than they were, and how promising things could be. After all, "*Tomorrow's just a dream away.*"

Leadership & You

As a leader, consider the following:

- Am I optimistic about the future?

- Is optimism a key factor in my hiring decisions?

- Do I expect optimism from others?

- What promises have I kept that have created a better world for others?

- What does a great big beautiful tomorrow look like to my

customers? My employees? How am I working to create that world?

- Do I see struggle as the road to opportunity?

- Do I seek to get up to bat as often as possible?

- Where has persistence paid off for me?

- Moving forward, how could persistence get me where I need to go?

3

IF YOU CAN DREAM IT, YOU CAN DO IT
LEADERS EXHIBIT A "CAN DO" ATTITUDE

The phrase "If you can dream it, you can do it" comes from a beloved Epcot attraction, Horizons. This ride-through experience spoke of visions of the past, present, and future. It suggests that if you can fully imagine something, you are then able to make that vision come alive.

I Think I Can, I Think I Can
LEADERS KNOW THEY CAN BECAUSE THEY THINK THEY CAN

It was the rallying cry of Casey Jr., the little circus train carrying Dumbo and the circus, over hill and valley, from one town to another. But his steam-filled declaration wasn't just a chant—it was the persistence in the work of chugging along. For us, it's an affirmative declaration for leaders who persist through their challenges. **Like Casey Jr., that "can do" persistence can get you over any hill and on to a brighter day.**

Parting the Water
LEADERS HAVE A "CAN DO" ATTITUDE

This is what Disney does. Collectively, the organization has nearly a century of experience in making the impossible possible. That possibility for making things happen begins with a great attitude. If anyone had a "Can do" attitude in the early days of Disneyland, it was Joe Fowler. His experience had been shaped by World War II, where he had supervised twenty-five shipyards. He knew what it meant to meet impossible deadlines. But he didn't have a clue what he was getting into with Walt Disney. Joe was from Los Gatos, in Northern California. On his initial visit to Disneyland, his expected two-day trip turned into three weeks. He ended up supervising construction of Disneyland and managing the park in Anaheim for ten years before going on to Walt Disney World in Florida.

One story is told of a conversation between Joe and Walt. Walt was designing a Polynesian luau show in Adventureland and he was discussing with Joe what he wanted the luau to look like. The stage would include a waterfall with a dressing room off to the side. Walt turned to Joe and said, "I'd like to part the water and let the entertainers come out and then have the waterfall close behind them." Joe never batted an eye. He just said, "Can do, can do."

No one was quite sure how Fowler was going to part the water, nor was anyone sure that Joe knew how, but he said it without hesitation—"can do." And indeed, he did pull it off.

Located on that same stage was a vinyl-leaf tree sculpted of cement, similar in style to what would become the Swiss Family Robinson Treehouse, and later Tarzan's Treehouse, only this one was smaller. The tree was so low to the ground that Walt asked if it could be raised. "Too low," Walt said. "Too late," said one engineer. "Too bad," said another.

But Joe stepped forward. He acknowledged that replacing the tree would be too expensive. So he suggested cutting the tree in the middle of the trunk and adding an additional section between the portion of the trunk leading to the roots and the other portion leading to the branches. The result would then lift the remainder of the tree. Walt got what he had requested because Joe made it happen.

On another occasion, Fowler parted the water to make the famed

Disneyland submarines a reality. Marty Sklar, former head of Disney Imagineering, notes in his biography, "When Bob Gurr handed his design for the Disneyland submarines to Joe Fowler, with no idea about how they could be built and with Walt questioning their feasibility, the admiral gave this response: 'Can do, Walt!' After the meeting, Bob Gurr asked Fowler how he could be so positive about building the submarines, based on Bob's simple sketch. **Joe Fowler responded: 'I don't have a clue, but we'll figure it out.' And 'we' did."**

Fowler was so trusted by Walt and Roy that he not only oversaw Disneyland, but was later charged with the enormous task of planning and building Walt Disney World. Wherever he went, the response was always the same, "Can Do."

"Canned" and "Can Do"
LEADERS BREAK THROUGH OBSTACLES

When you know how to make the future happen, you expect others will help do the same. Indeed, leaders expect the positive in others. To that end, Walt encouraged others to be positive and optimistic. Conversely, he held little patience toward those who would drag others down. Jim Algar, studio director, stated: "When you worked around Walt, everything was yes answers or hopeful answers. He never, for a minute, entertained a 'no' answer. **He [Walt] didn't suffer people who were cynics or skeptics, because they got in his way."**

Early on in the planning of Disneyland, engineers emphasized the need for a water tower to supply pressure for fire hydrants and sprinklers. Walt wanted neither water towers nor power lines on nearby properties. "Find another solution" was his demand. In the end, they piped water in from more than one source, assuring an unchanging pressure. They also relocated power lines. It all cost money, but it was important to Walt's vision of what Disneyland would become.

This same expectation played out in managing the park. C. V. Wood was a charismatic man hired to build and run Disneyland. He became Disneyland's first executive vice president. Wood was actually the executive who brought the aforementioned Joe Fowler into the company. Yet, the two were in many ways opposites. As we mentioned earlier in the chapter, Fowler was a "can do" sort of man who knew how to make things happen, pace himself, and meet a deadline. He was accustomed to keeping people informed and consistently assured Walt that the park would open on time.

C. V., on the other hand, was less than optimistic about the park opening on time, and tried at one point to get Walt to simply board up Tomorrowland entirely for the opening. Throughout construction, he expressed skepticism that the park would open on time. He even pushed for a later opening in September. Joe Fowler countered that they would lose the vacation months if they did and might not ever recover afterwards.

Fowler was right. Physically, Joe would get the park open on time. But C. V. Wood's management in getting the park operationally up and running toward opening day created much of what caused the "Black Sunday" issues. Walt could see that C. V. had failed to take care of the details that Wood himself said he would. Moreover, Walt didn't have patience for Wood's attitude.

Animosity continued between C. V. and the Disney brothers. Two weeks after the park opened, Walt and C. V. had a major argument over why the Maxwell Coffee House remained uncompleted. When Walt returned to California from a trip, he learned the delay was a result of decisions made by Maxwell House officials and Disneyland food and beverage personnel. The problem could have been avoided if Wood had been more thorough in his negotiations.

Walt was tired of C. V. not being able to work with others to make it happen. He told Roy that he wanted Wood out of there. Roy agreed, though he himself had originally hired Wood. Then Roy discovered that Wood had granted merchandising rights at

Disneyland to an unknown souvenir company at a fraction of the actual cost. This resulted in a loss of potential revenue for the organization. Such a finding verified both Walt and Roy's instinct for terminating Wood.

In his research, Bob Thomas notes that after Roy removed C. V. Wood, it would still be years later and after lengthy legal research before they would find out that C. V. Wood and a buddy had quietly set up a company that they had hoped would monopolize the merchandise business. It begs the question: **Can anyone remain positive if their behavior is perhaps in conflict with their values?**

Walt simply had no tolerance for those who didn't have a "can do" attitude. Bill Martin recalls his experience with Walt: "I came from Fox Studios, and when they asked me a question there, I told them what I thought, so I did that when I went to work for Disney. I guess Walt appreciated some outside thinking. He did teach me not to be too dogmatic about my suggestions. I found that out in a hurry."

Martin remembered a certain artist who had designed a ride and when the artist told Walt: "You know, if you can't do it this way, I don't know how you're going to do it." He was fired the next day. "Walt didn't want to hear that kind of talk," Martin recalled. "You could do anything if you wanted. **Walt used to say, 'I don't care what you can't do. I want to hear what you can do.'** If there were fifteen ways to solve a problem, Walt was looking at all fifteen. He was a taskmaster, but he made it interesting, and he'd give you a little charge to go ahead and do it the way you liked it best. Then he would comment on that."

"No-Way" in Norway
LEADERS FIND OPPORTUNITIES WHERE OTHERS FAIL

Conversely, Fowler's example is so remembered, that if you pass the central construction shops at Walt Disney World, you'll see a big sign out front with the words: "The Can Do People." This notion especially played out in the construction of Norway, one of the World Showcase countries at Epcot. Prior to this time, the folks at Central Shops had done much of the work. The skilled carpenters, welders, painters, and other craftsman built much of what had become Walt Disney World at that time, to include the Magic Kingdom and Epcot Center. That was especially needed because most of that kind of talent was not widely available in Central Florida when the resort was initially built.

But in the 1980s, there was not only a lot of talent to be found in and around the Orlando area, but with increasing costs, it seemed to Disney management that it only made sense to "shop around" for the best deal.

Therefore, the Central Shops, who had come to expect to be the group responsible for such work at Disney, now had to compete for doing that work. One of the first projects they lost in the bidding war was building the Maelstrom boat attraction.

The definition for Maelstrom can be a large, powerful whirlpool, but it can also be used to define a confused act of turmoil. So the title probably was well selected, because outsourced parties fell way behind in their ability to build a dependable, solid, Disney-standard attraction. It wasn't long before insiders were referring to the Norway ride as the "No-Way" ride. In the end, Central Shops came to the rescue, making the attraction one that would go on to operate for years to come.

That's not to say that an outside contractor can't do a fantastic job. But what matters is that whoever is on the job has a "can do" attitude about making the dream a reality. Here's an example of how that "can do" attitude—or lack thereof—can impact your future.

The Link Between Dreaming & Doing
LEADERS EXERCISE PATIENCE

If there's a key ingredient that takes people from dreaming it to doing it that keeps them in that "can do" place, it would be passion. But what is passion? Is it a splash of zealousness, or a deep river of patience? One doesn't typically think of patience as being synonymous with passion. To quote author Mark Z. Danielewski:

> **Passion has little to do with euphoria and everything to do with patience.** It is not about feeling good. It is about endurance. Like patience, passion comes from the same Latin root: pati. It does not mean to flow with exuberance. It means to suffer.

We've noted that endurance and persistence earlier in the life of Walt Disney. And yet patience and suffering is not what people want to sign up for when it comes to making their dreams a reality. Indeed, patience often conjures up the notion of having to put up with bureaucratic barriers and obstacles that keep us from making those dreams a reality. Turkish author Elif Shafak wrote:

"Patience does not mean to passively endure. It means to be farsighted enough to trust the end result of a process. What does patience mean? It means to look at the thorn and see the rose, to look at the night and see the dawn. Impatience means to be so shortsighted as to not be able to see the outcome."

Here's a great example of someone who has made dreams come true at Disney. In the story below, you'll see the tale of a man who exercised the patience requisite to truly being passionate. And yet, his dreams came true in ways that perhaps were better than he even imagined.

Being Better Than Disney
LEADERS FIND WAYS TO DO IT BETTER

There are many individuals who, over the decades, have acted on a vision, delivering real magic for Disney. Here's one who did just that—outside of Disney. As a child, Garner Holt was so amazed by a *Wonderful World of Disney* episode of the Haunted Mansion, that he decided he would create animatronics for a living. Long story short, he now makes amazing animatronics, parade floats, and other fantastic scenery and theming elements. Do you like the Little Mermaid attraction at Magic Kingdom and Disney California Adventure? *The Nightmare Before Christmas* in Haunted Mansion Holiday? The characters that come to life in Hong Kong Disneyland's Mystic Manor? Do you enjoy seeing the cars come to life at Radiator Springs Racers? Do you like everything that moves when you hit it on Buzz Lightyear Astro Blasters? That's the work of Garner Holt and his team.

And yet, the twist is that Garner has never been an Imagineer. Nor has he ever been an official Disney Cast Member. He's what you call an outside contractor, or as Disney likes to put it, an operating partner. He has operated on this premise: **Do Disney so much better than Disney that you essentially become Disney**. And with that, he gets to do some of the most amazing and fun projects–not just for Disney, but also for many other parks, restaurants, and exhibits.

Of course, that didn't happen overnight. It took years of perfecting his own animatronic creations. It took lonely years of small projects with local malls before anyone at Disney really took him seriously. But he persisted patiently. In the end, Disney not only saw the need for Garner's creations, they realized that his operation could produce them in-house better and more economically than Disney. So, over time, Garner Holt has received more and more work. And now today, so many of the animatronics that Guests love at the Disney parks are really due to a man who has never worn a Disney nametag, but who defines quality at Disney.

It offers an important point—The reality you dream of making happen may not necessarily happen the way you initially conceived it. But it can happen—and in some ways, it may happen in ways you never dreamed possible. Opportunity sometimes favors possibilities beyond your finest dreams. So definitely dream it. But be prepared for doing it in ways you never would have thought of previously.

Whatever you want to do with your life, know that you can become so much better than the very best in your business. It's not easy, but it can be done. To that end, take Garner's advice—put in enough perseverance and focus on your dreams, and they will come true. **Know that if you work hard enough and smart enough, you may end up doing Disney so much better than Disney that you may become...well...Disney.**

Leadership & You

As a leader, consider the following:

- How can a "can do" attitude help me to compete with others in the workplace?

- What improvements can I make that will better serve the customer experience, as well as the bottom line?

- How do I build the confidence to tackle big projects?

- How long am I willing to keep going, while uncertain about whether something is going to be successful?

- Am I passionate? Does my passion provide you the patience to see my dreams through to becoming a reality?

4

HEIGH-HO, HEIGH-HO, IT'S OFF TO WORK WE GO
LEADERS WORK HARD

It's the anthem of the seven dwarfs. Those same fellows went on to sing, *"It ain't no trick to get rich quick if you dig dig dig with a shovel or pick."* This chapter looks at what kind of digging is involved to create success, because work is the primary ingredient in making dreams come true.

Giving Away Our Secrets!
LEADERS WORK HARDER THAN THEIR COMPETITORS

There's a little known story told to me by my first supervisor, Valerie Oberle, who was the original leader of The Disney University Professional Development Programs, an institution that would eventually become known as The Disney Institute. It seems that back in the days of Michael Eisner and Frank Wells, Michael was concerned that programs would be giving away all of Disney's "secrets" to other companies all over the world. Michael was concerned that we were giving away "the secret formula." So Michael and Frank showed up unannounced to a program one day at the old Walt Disney World Conference Center to actually view one of the programs being delivered.

After observing for some 40 minutes, they walked out of the room. Michael was anxious and wanted to shut the programs down. "See…they're giving away our secrets!" But Frank, always the calming influence, reassured Michael that giving away their "secrets" shouldn't worry him. Why? Because the secret at Disney, according to Frank Wells, is that **"we work very, very, very hard to pull off what we do, and no one else has that kind of discipline to do so."**

With that reasoning, Michael seemed pacified, and the business programs of the Disney Institute continued on.

The Art of Work
LEADERS EXERCISE DISCIPLINE

As mentioned earlier, "If you can dream it, you can do it." While oft quoted, many don't think long and hard enough about what that quotation means. Most draw the conclusion that anything you are capable of doing anything you can dream of. Perhaps if we turn this quote around, we might see this quotation with new eyes: **"If you can do it, it's because you really dreamed through it."** The suggestion here is that those who have the focus and discipline to do something new also have the focus and discipline to really dream through the impossible.

Here's another perspective on this. Al Hirschfield was well known as the American caricaturist who celebrated Broadway's best through drawing. To Disney fans, Al's work was the inspiration for the New York setting in George Gershwin's "Rhapsody in Blue" scene in *Fantasia 2000*. As one who knew something about art and creativity all his life, he made the following statement:

"I believe everybody is creative and everybody is talented. I just don't think that everybody is disciplined. I think that's a rare commodity."

Perhaps there is not only a discipline for making dreams come true, but in coming up with the dream itself. Anyone can come up with ideas, but a dream come true is a true mental creation. Do you have ideas? Do you dream of doing something great? Have you labored over that dream until it is a mental creation in your mind? Stephen R. Covey talks about the physical creation following the mental, just as a building follows a blueprint. Dreams take real effort!

If doing requires dreaming, what is needed for dreaming to take place? Walt Disney stated, **"All your dreams can come true if you have the courage to pursue them."** Why courage? Does that mean that if I'm cowardly, I can't dream? What does courage have to do with dreaming? Someone once said that the opposite of courage in our society is not cowardice. It is conformity. I think what Walt was saying is that if you want your dreams to come true, you have to have courage to make it happen, and not just conform to what is currently all around you. If you think about it, probably the best dreamers and doers are the ones who do not settle for what is. They dream because they see the possibilities in what could be.

Walt lived his life not just doing, but dreaming as well. In the stories mentioned before, Walt had the courage to get on the train and come out to Hollywood in hopes of making a new start. He dreamed new dreams then took courage to make them a reality. And that courage required work.

Kicking it In Gear
LEADERS BALANCE PRIORITIES WITHOUT MAKE EXCUSES

In an article in *Variety*, Bob Iger speaks of a former boss, Roone Arledge, a leader he admired for the results he achieved. Roone was a key part of ABC's rise in the networks by providing leadership to both ABC Sports and ABC News. Describing Roone, Iger noted:

> He demanded perfection. I both respected and loved him—but there were times when I thought that what he was asking of us was just either not possible or not human. It didn't matter how much time you had left; it didn't matter if [people] had to stay up all night. It didn't matter

if it was their birthday, their anniversary, their kid's bar mitzvah, whatever it was. You went in and you did it. And at some point you did it for him, too, because you appreciated what he was trying to accomplish.

So when asked if Iger would want to take a different approach, he goes on to note:

> If someone comes to you with, "It's my kid's graduation," you don't tell them, "Sorry, you can't go to that." You just can't do that. You figure out some other way.
>
> But I'm amazed how many times someone says, "Well, we just can't make it better" or, "We're out of time" or whatever. **Saying no becomes such a cheap and easy way out.** [My response is], "Wait a minute, yes you can." Or, "How about trying as hard as you can?"

Bob Iger sees the need for balance and for working with an individual's personal needs. But he also sees that there are too often excuses, and that those excuses keep people from really accomplishing the impossible. Leaders balance their priorities without making excuses.

An Imagineer in the Kitchen
LEADERS LEARN WHAT THEY DON'T KNOW

Trying as hard as you can is essential to making the dream a reality. So is taking the initiative without being asked to do so. John Hench worked for the company for sixty-five years. His tenure was so long at Disney that he was called upon as an artist to design his own awards for tenure, as no one else had reached those milestones! So many attractions bear his influence, like Spaceship Earth, Carousel of Progress, and even Cinderella Castle.

According to Marty Sklar's book, *Dream It! Do It! My Half Century*

Creating Disney's Magic Kingdoms, John was assigned by Walt Disney to redesign Disneyland's Victorian-style Plaza Inn restaurant. By the 1960s, John Hench had been an artist working on films like *Fantasia, Dumbo,* and *Peter Pan.* He had even earned an Oscar for his special effects work on a certain squid in *20,000 Leagues Under the Sea.* But one thing John had never done was work in a restaurant.

John Hench protested to Walt Disney about working on a restaurant, noting that he knew nothing about that business. Walt's response was, "Well, find out!"

So John enrolled in a course on restaurant management being offered at UCLA. He learned about the business. He not only succeeded in designing a restaurant that stands the test of time, he became the design staff's authority on back-of-house restaurant structuring and requirements. That's how John led his life. He passed away in 2004 at age 95, still working full-time for Disney.

Walt's message: If you don't know how to do it, learn it!

Then be sure to make the deadline!

Making Epcot's Deadline
LEADERS MAKE DEADLINES

While the expression "If you can dream it, you can do it" is what Guests remember, the opening crew remembered something much more like: "We have dreamed it, now we must do it!" Dick Nunis was at what was known as EPCOT Center throughout the construction, installation, and start-up process. Each day, the key leaders met with him for an on-site progress report. Art Frohwerk, responsible for overseeing much of the engineering work done by the Imagineers attended via radio as "Engineering 1." In these sessions, Art was quick to observe who was surviving and who was crumbling. Dick held everyone's feet to the fire—those who promised the world and then didn't deliver would often walk out feeling like their skin was peeled off. These sessions became even more intense as the October 1st opening date neared.

Art learned to come to the sessions ready to listen to concerns, be open to ideas, suggest alternative solutions, make commitments, and address the realities. This earned him the respect he needed from Dick and other key leaders and allowed him to get favors when he needed it most.

One such favor came just a week prior to opening. There was a lot of stress among those who were laboring over Spaceship Earth, but several attractions had challenges incorporating the technology. Many engineers and technicians were doing amazing work debugging the last minute details of these large-scale integrated systems.

The pressure was on as never before. Engineering 1 (Art) was called on the radio one afternoon and was asked to come to the south end of Spaceship Earth. There, the executives met to talk about the impossible conditions of Spaceship Earth. Testing and demo work was still going on, there were too many loose ends, and nothing seemed to work at the same time. Art was informed that the AT&T sponsor was coming in at 10 a.m. the next day and wanted to ride the attraction. Art was asked to give it his personal attention since the lead ride engineer assigned to the attraction was burnt out.

Art started talking to each of the various team members involved in order to figure out what was going to make it work quickly and reliably. The engineers were under tremendous stress—Art discovered that the engineer responsible for the audio had experienced a near nervous breakdown. This individual held technical knowledge that no one else had. Art asked one of the other show designers to help him out. Seeing that they were going to labor all night to make this happen, Art made a call to Dick's office and asked for a favor—could he have the kitchens provide enough cheeseburgers, fries, and drinks to get them through the evening—delivered at 1:00 a.m.?

Late into the evening, everyone was focused on getting the show up and running. Art walked up and down the ride talking to the crews. **The problem with getting Spaceship Earth up and running wasn't whether anything would work; it was whether everything would work at the same time**. Animation people were busily costuming show figures, lighting was still being set, show designers were giving last minute directives, and mechanical techs were crawling all over the track and taking apart the drive system to replace parts.

Then, 1:00 a.m. came and all these cheeseburgers, fries, and drinks appeared. Soon it looked like a picnic up and down all 18 floors of the ride corridor. Workers who were never treated to much of anything were talking about this as being the place to be. Mechanics were relaxing and joking for the first time in weeks. The audio engineer came in and seemed to have a smile, if just for a minute.

By 9:00 a.m. the next morning, the ride was up and running. The sponsor arrived 15 minutes early and boarded the ride. Past the Pharaoh, under the Sistine Chapel, and into outer space—it worked beautifully. The team had succeeded under pressure.

No one likes deadlines. But if you can find passion in patience as was mentioned earlier, maybe you can also find passion in a deadline. So is the experience in our next story.

Leadership & You

As a leader, consider the following:

- Am I really trying hard? What demonstrates my commitment to doing the work that will realize my dreams?

- Do I work very, very hard to accomplish those goals?

- Are there things I can't do, that I simply must make the effort to learn?

- Can I make deadlines—no matter who imposes them on me?

- When I don't know how to do something, do I take the self-initiative to find out how?

- How do I work despite the obstacles and circumstances I am in?

- How do I make it easier for my employees to accomplish the work?

- What are the "cheeseburgers and fries" that morally support my team in the hour of need?

5

I'M LATE! I'M LATE!
FOR A VERY IMPORTANT DATE!
LEADERS OPTIMIZE TIME

Those words caught Alice's attention in the film, *Alice in Wonderland*. Here she was casually enjoying a moment in a meadow when a rabbit with a waistcoat and a pocket watch hastily hurried by, exclaiming he was late for a very important date. The rhythmic phrase is recited by a great many who find they have lost track of time and are running behind.

There's another expression found in the story: Down the rabbit hole. Curious about the white rabbit, Alice follows him down the rabbit hole. And thus, her experience begins.

Going down a rabbit hole is an idiom often used in society. It suggests moving along a path that increasingly becomes more confounding and complicated. When it comes to managing time, it's about more than just being late. There are a few rabbit holes you may want to avoid by optimizing your use of time.

- You make the wrong impression by not showing up on time.
- You fail to bring your passion to the table.
- You fail to deliver on time.
- You end up being late to market on a timely basis.
- Your efforts with controlling time frames makes you start to come across as obsessive compulsive.

The following offers examples both good and bad that illustrate these points.

Bob Iger: Be on Time
LEADERS ARE ON TIME

A company like Disney in many ways runs...well...like a company. So what does the head of Disney think about managing time? In a Fortune 6 Magazine article, CEO Bob Iger confided that in addition to waking up at 4:30 seven days a week and exercising, he starts meetings on time.

> "I'm zealous about that because my day needs to be managed like clockwork. If people are late for meetings, the meetings tend to go late, which throws off my agenda thereafter. I frequently start the meeting even if all the people expected to be in attendance aren't there. I don't need to say to people, 'Be on time.' They know."

Timing & Time
LEADERS MAKE IT TO MARKET AT THE RIGHT TIME AND PLACE

One of the definitive icons of the Walt Disney Company is the Mickey Mouse Watch. This timepiece is as much about timing than it is about time.

As the depression loomed, Walt Disney was looking for new revenue sources on top of the *Mickey Mouse* and *Silly Symphonies* shorts. The thought was that licensing Mickey Mouse to merchandise might be an answer to that. Herman "Kay" Kamen was an advertising man from Kansas City and he thought he could sell Mickey Mouse in a new and better way than what was being done at the time. Kay headed to California on a train to meet with Walt. A contract soon followed which allowed Kay to be the company's sole licensing representative.

When President Herbert Hoover promised a chicken in every pot, Kay Kamen promised a Disney character in every home. Within three years, the different kinds of Mickey Mouse products stood numbered in the thousands. But one product uniquely stood out. During this same time, Ingersoll-Waterbury Clock Company was facing bankruptcy. Kay struck up a deal with the fledgling company to sell watches priced at $3.25. Again, timing was everything. The watches were a massive hit. Macy's department store in New York City sold a record 11,000 watches in one day. The Ingersoll Waterbury company had to increase the number of factory workers from 300 to 3,000.

Watches continued to be successful, not just Mickey, but Minnie and many others. And then of course, there was the Goofy watch. The numbers were put in backwards, with Goofy's hands going around counter clockwise. Yes, they were difficult to read, but they were extremely popular.

The rest is history. Disney products in that early era provided the fuel to help Walt's studio develop its first animated feature, *Snow White and the Seven Dwarfs*. Previous to the show's opening, Kay had some 117 manufacturers licensed to sell products from the film. Of course, Disney products are everywhere today. Hundreds of Disney stores are scattered across the United States and abroad. Theme parks sell merchandise at the exit to nearly every attraction and park. Major properties include not just Mickey and Minnie, but Star Wars, *Frozen*, Disney Princess, Cars, Spider-Man, Avengers, Winnie the Pooh, and other Disney classics. In truth, managing time is about being at the right place at the right time.

MATADORS to the Rescue
LEADERS DELIVER ON TIME WHEN OTHERS CAN'T

You've probably heard the expression, "luck favors the prepared."

Well, time favors the prepared as well.

Walt Disney noted: "Everyone needs deadlines. Even the beavers. They loaf around all summer, but when they are faced with the winter deadline, they work like fury. If we didn't have deadlines, we'd stagnate."

Disney is rife with tales about barely making deadlines:

- Fantasia made its opening night debut with only two hours to spare. While completing the final scene of Ave Maria, an earthquake shook the studio causing the production team to need to start over again. The final reel barely made the premiere.

- As mentioned earlier, Disneyland barely opened to crowds on July 17th, 1955 with attractions still not prepared, drinking fountains still not plumbed, and women's heels sinking into the fresh asphalt. It not only survived, but thrived, but not without receiving the title on opening day of "Black Sunday."

- The opening of Epcot was planned for October 1st, 1982. But when the contractor was asked if they were going to open on October 1st, the response was, "I'm okay with October 1st. It's 1982 that concerns me!"

One of my favorite stories comes from *Spinning Disney's World*, a memoir by Charles Ridgway, who served as Disney's press agent. The story speaks of a can-do team who was willing to do what it took to make a deadline. Charlie headed up a team organized by Michael Eisner called The MATADORS (Marketing and Admissions Team Assigned to Disney Objectives of Rapidly Succeeding) Because so little had traditionally been done in terms of mass marketing prior to Eisner, this team was responsible for creating new promotional opportunities for the company. The Rockettes coming to Walt Disney World and Disney-shaped hot air balloons sailing across the country were examples of this.

Perhaps the MATADORS' biggest accomplishment came on the eve of Mickey's 60th birthday. The original thought was to do the typical bunting, signage, and parade. Some additional brainstorming came in, adding a birthday tent in the parking lot behind Main Street, and then offering a bunch of birthday-related activities.

The idea of building Mickey's Birthdayland was outlined to Imagineers who were immersed in building out the Disney-MGM Studios. They pushed back on the last-minute workload. Disappointed, the MATADORS took their idea to the "Can Do" maintenance planning team dedicated to projects at Walt Disney World. From there, the idea grew to creating the event in an unused corner sandwiched between Fantasyland and Tomorrowland with Mickey's house acting as the centerpiece. Also conceived was the idea of adding a train station and re-theming that to Mickey's Birthday Express.

In February of that year, the MATADORS got permission from Eisner to create the new Birthdayland. A budget of $12 million was set aside–a modest amount considering that Splash Mountain was built during that same period for nearly ten times that amount. The only challenge was that Eisner insisted that the project be completed by summer so it would support increased attendance that season.

Construction started the day after approval and the time frame was tight. There were many components to the project. Guests would be welcomed to Duckburg with a population in the "bill"ions. There was Grandma Duck's farm with a Minnie Moo, a cow who had a Mickey Mouse silhouette on one side of her body. There was also a modest playground and an inflatable of Mickey. There was even Mickey's House–a place you could walk through and visit.

Yet probably what people remembered most were the circus tents rising up into the sky. Entertainment came in with three big circus-style tents just for the birthday show–one for the queue, one for the show itself, and one for a "Happy Birthday" finale/retail space. Then they also erected a fourth tent fronted by a theater marquee as a space to go and see Mickey Mouse in his own dressing room. They reasoned that if it were Mickey's birthday, a lot of people would want to get a picture with him. So they created a dedicated space that "magically" optimized the number of people who could see Mickey in the same moment.

Amazingly, the project opened that summer, with Nancy Reagan being guest of honor at the dedication. Though it went over budget by a couple of million, it was so popular and so well received, that after the birthday, management kept the entire land, making modest cosmetic changes and re-titling it as Mickey's Starland.

In the wake of this success, Imagineers finally got on board by further expanding the idea and opening an entire Toontown in 1993 at Disneyland in California. Then looking back at the Magic Kingdom, they knew they needed to do something more. In the years following, the structure created for the land to serve as a temporary attraction had long worn out its welcome. It was time to do something different.

As a Cast Member, I was there at 3:30 in the morning on October 1, 1996 when Mickey's Toontown Fair was being hosed down and prepared for the first Guests that morning. In the distance you could see a glowing Cinderella Castle in the form of a birthday cake for the whole park. But the real changes on that day were here in this corner of the park. In fact, after the re-dedication ceremonies that day, I went home, picked up my wife and little ones, and took them out to the park so they could see the new land outfitted for the Fab Five. Included were Minnie's House, Goofy's Barnstormer, Donald's Boat, a new playground, and new meet and greet locations for not only Mickey, but other Disney characters as well. One of the four tents was taken away, but there were still three remaining. Rather than creating a Toontown like at Disneyland, Imagineers re-engineered the tents and played up the concept of a fair-type experience. Other than the tents and the train station, little of the original Birthdayland/Starland remained. Even Mickey's House was completely reshaped to be more cartoon-like in its appearance, with few, if any, 90-degree angles.

Millions visited Mickey's Toontown Fair over the years. Still, it wasn't like Toontown at Disneyland. There was still a lack of permanence. With the new Fantasyland expansion came the opportunity to re-look at this corner of the Magic Kingdom. The idea was to take the circus tent and Goofy's Barnstormer and merge it with Dumbo's Flying Elephants—something that was not really a part of the medieval fare of Fantasyland. Of the four original tents, only two remain, but another two have been created, one for Dumbo's queue and another for miscellaneous purposes. The earlier tents have been redone and they provide a meet 'n greet along with a retail location, all with a Dumbo-style circus flair. The time period is decidedly late 30s/early 40s, the same period as when Dumbo was first released. Today, we now have Storybook Circus.

If it had not been for the imagination and persistence of the MATADORS along with the hard work of the maintenance team at Walt Disney World, we probably wouldn't have that corner of the park today. Disney parks are complicated attractions, something that doesn't afford a quick-turn around. But in that short creative space, magic was made overnight that created new kinds of experiences we still enjoy today.

So it is that being resourceful requires working with limited resources, labor, and even time. But it's more than that. It's about finding your passion and focus in that deadline.

Aulani: Finding Passion in a Deadline
LEADERS FIND THEIR PASSION IN A DEADLINE

When you visit Aulani, you enter through an open lobby. Stepping inside, there are two forces vying for your attention. The first is the view of beautifully landscaped grounds with its volcano and the ocean beyond the lobby porch. Restraining you from moving toward this point is a striking 360-degree mural done by Martin Charlot. His father, Jean Charlot, had lectured to Disney artists many years prior.

There were requirements made on this mural. One was that Charlot wanted the whole mural to be about Hawaii before Captain Cook discovered the islands. Joe Rohde, head of Imagineering for the project, was fine with the idea, but he also required that the side of the mural leaning toward the ocean be about modern Hawaii.

The second requirement was that he get it done in time. Charlot explains it this way:

> "There was, though, another very real pressure that ruled my artistic output and that was time. I had miniature canvases that I had made on which I was going to design the mural composition. When I had all 24 full size canvas panels stretched and delivered to my apartment/studio, I felt a click go off in my brain. It was like a stopwatch clicking telling me there was no time left to make sketches of the mural composition. That brain clock was right on as I finished the mural, after two years of work, one week before it had to be sent to Hawaii to be installed. Meeting the deadline meant painting every day from morning to night, no time to sketch, no time to doodle, just paint and paint again."

You would think that such deadlines would stifle an artist. But listen to what Charlot goes on to say: "Every day was an artist's dream—do my thing, painting, over and over again. That meant trusting my instinct, running on automatic every day. I loved it."

Very few people think of a time limitation as being a stimulus toward creativity, much less toward loving one's work. Usually, we walk away after a deadline hating the thing all the more because we had to rush to get it done. But in this case, Martin Charlot drew on not only his skills, but also his passion in creating what is truly an amazing piece of art. You will be stunned when you visit Aulani, for it is truly a beautiful piece.

For those of us who use pens and laptops instead of paints and brushes, think about your upcoming deadline and how you can draw your own passion and strengths in meeting the time frame. Does time limit your creativity, or can it free you up to focus fully and solely on your passion? Don't count how much time you have left. Make every moment you have left count!

Between a Rock and a Deadline with Mickey
LEADERS TAKE OWNERSHIP AND ACCOUNTABILITY FOR
THEIR TIMELINES

What happens when deadlines are tight? Can you really afford to
let people be empowered, take responsibility, and take the lead
themselves? This can be really difficult, especially when you report
to Mickey. Not Mickey Mouse. Mickey Steinberg.
Skip Lange was the quintessential rockwork expert. His
responsibility was to take care of all rock structures during the
construction of Disneyland Paris. That included Skull Rock in
Adventureland, alien rock croppings in Tomorrowland, and
grandest of all, Big Thunder Mountain Railroad. On one
occasion, he felt very beat up by Mickey Steinberg in a meeting.
Mickey, as the number 2 guy at Imagineering, was in Paris to
make sure the project was completed on time. Skip left the
meeting hurt by the conversation, but then returned to converse
privately with Mickey. There, he noted that it wasn't fair that he
was being blamed for things that were not under his control.

Mickey called everyone back into the meeting and announced
that Skip Lange would be completely in charge of all rockwork.
He instructed everyone that Skip would decide how the rockwork
was to be planned, managed, and executed. Then turning to Skip,
he said, "Now Mr. Lange, you know what this means. I will not be
coming to any of them about rockwork any more, I will be
coming to *you*. Do you understand?" With that, Skip took over
rockwork and made it happen.

That was how Mickey rolled; he empowered you, gave you the
support, but then expected results. When speaking of that same
park project, a *Season Pass Podcast* interview illustrated how Mickey
Steinberg replaced another Imagineer with Mark Eades as show
producer and project manager to get Le Visionarium open in
time. This attraction was signature to the park, as it fulfilled a
requirement made of Disney to create an attraction that built off
of the heritage of France.

It was August. The park was supposed to open in April. The

schedule was very tight when Mark was put on the project. And Mickey, in announcing that Mark would take over, stated in his gentlemanly southern drawl how behind the project was, and then declared: "...and Mark, if you don't deliver this on time, you'll be fired." That was Mickey's way of saying Mark was in charge of this ticking bomb.

On the same day as the announcement, Mark beat a hasty retreat, taking the project scheduler with him. They went to a Bob's Big Boy nearby in Glendale. There they spent the next four hours re-configuring the schedule by working backwards.

The next day he held a meeting with all of the key people. There, the new schedule was passed out to everyone. Stars were listed next to names on the schedule. When asked what the stars meant, Mark turned to the team to clarify:

> "Here's how we're going to do this project. If you see a star next to your name, you know that you are the one responsible for that particular activity on the schedule. Failure to make a decision, you forfeit your right to make any more decisions for the project from that day forward—and I will make them for you."

No one wanting Mark Eades to make the decisions quickly led to everyone making their deadlines. It was tense and difficult, but they had the show completed a week prior to opening.

Empowering people is trusting them to deliver results. It is not easy. But it's critical to working in a sustained way with teams. Done right, it yields not only trust, but greater morale. Taking the right steps for cultivating that morale is where we go next.

Time management matters. Leaders have to use time as a resource if they hope to really accomplish their work. Being late to a meeting can introduce some temporary challenges. Being habitually late demonstrates that you are either not committed to the work you do, or you lack discipline. Again, take responsibility and authority given to you to make your deadlines. Otherwise, you're likely to end up down a rabbit hole.

Leadership & You

As a leader, consider the following:

- Do you have the discipline to show up on time?

- How is your timing?

- Can you scramble to meet tight deadlines? How do you organize to do so?

- What are you doing to not be late to market?

- Can you find passion in a deadline?

- How do you hold others accountable for managing their time?

- Do you have a practical sense about managing your time?

6

IT'S WHATCHA DO WITH WHATCHA GOT
LEADERS ARE RESOURCEFUL

Many people think that an organization like Disney is so rich that it can do anything it wants to. Spending money is not a problem. But the fact of the matter is–organizations always have to pay attention to the bottom line. Ultimately, there is someone you must be accountable to when it comes to how you use your assets. And it isn't just about the money. Sometimes it can be about being more resourceful with your time or energy.

The Disney Studios struggled in the wake of World War II. Indeed, much of the 1940s were a very lean time for the organization, as it was difficult to get into certain markets, and much of the labor during the war had gone off to fight.
To get by, a modest film called *So Dear to My Heart* was produced during this time. The lyrics of a song in this film provides us context:

> *It's whatcha do with whatcha got*
> *And never mind just how muchya got*
> *It's whatcha do with whatcha got*
> *That pays off in the end.*

> *You gotta start with what you got*
> *And whatcha got ain't such a lot,*
> *To make the most of what you got,*
> *Here's what I recommend:*

> *You start by a tryin' and applyin' your best*
> *If you try, there ain't no denyin'*

71

There's a way to feather your nest.
You gotta add how mucha do
And multiply by whatcha do.
You think you can't win, butcha do
And you get back dividend.

The song was penned in the 1940s, but the spirit of that song began some two decades earlier. It began in something as simple as a garage.

Garage Greatness
LEADERS EMERGE FROM HUMBLE BEGINNINGS

Besides working with computers, what do Steve Jobs and Steve Wozniak of Apple, as well as Bill Hewlett and David Packard, all have in common?

You find that answer in part at the top of Spaceship Earth. As our "time machines" in the ride emerge to the present, we see a family watching Apollo 11 land on the moon, followed by an office housing large computers.

Narrator Judi Dench speaks of the landing on the moon by noting:

> To send a man to the moon, we had to invent a new language, spoken not by man, but by computers. At first, very large, very expensive computers, but we see the potential. What if everyone could have one of these amazing computers in their own house? There's just one problem--they're as big as a house. The solution comes in, of all places, a garage in California.

We then emerge to a garage scene where our narrator notes, "Young people with a passion for shaping the future put the power of the computer in everyone's hands."

Pam Fisher, Imagineer and the show's writer, explains:

> We all looked at that scene as an homage to...the
> innovation (that) happened in garages of California.
> There's a lot of this notion of young people in Northern
> California (working) on kitchen tables, in garages, making
> the personal computer possible.

The answer is that Hewlett and Packard, as well as Jobs and
Wozniak, started phenomenal companies in a garage. But they're
not the only ones. Walt Disney also started in a garage. Elliot and
Ruth Handler of Mattel did too. For that matter, C.E. Woolman
started what became Delta Airlines out of a gas-station garage and
DeWitt and Lila Wallace nurtured *Reader's Digest* from a garage
apartment.

It isn't that there is something inherent in the physical aesthetic of
a garage; they simply act as an incubator for possibilities. Stripped
down to the bare essentials, one becomes focused on building
upward and onward. **The idea of working from a garage
suggests a state of mind and a rejection of the status quo
in search of something that will be the next big thing.** It
fosters a spirit of entrepreneurship that sometimes can't be
addressed in the trappings of a fine office building.

Clearly, you have to provide people the resources necessary to do
their job. That means the right hardware and software in terms of
furnishings and tools. It also means placing them in an
environment that supports the culture you want to create. Still,
sometimes the best setting is the one that focuses you on what you
want to accomplish, rather than supplying the comforts and
luxuries that keep you distracted. Sometimes the best setting is one
that makes you hungry for something better.

Being resourceful is more than offices and supplies. It also has to
do with your labor. At Disney, it's when all hands are "on deck."

Green Side Up When Naming the Sheriff
LEADERS JUMP IN AND HELP

I was present when Dick Nunis once told the now familiar story about the opening of Walt Disney World. The night before the press opening of Walt Disney World, students from Rollins College had been called in to help with tasks for getting the resort ready. With the clock running out, Dick Nunis was out in front of the Contemporary Resort directing these kids to get the sod laid out in patches. Some had never laid sod and asked for greater direction. Dick's reply was, "Green Side Up!"

This was the way things were often done during that time. An even better example of this comes not from the Contemporary Resort, but from the streets of Frontierland. In the olden days, frontier towns were kept at peace by a sheriff who oversaw law and order. Often the sheriff was called upon to carry out tough duties others feared accomplishing. In that role, they often carried out jobs beyond policing. Those duties included keeping watch over the jail, removing straying animals, or playing judge.

In his book, *Spinning Disney's World*, Charles Ridgway talks about how Walt Disney would call on individuals to handle specific assignments that were beyond the call of duty. **Walt tapped into individuals to get something done even though it was clearly not part of their expertise. He called it "Naming the Sheriff."**

After Walt, the title stayed on. For example, take a look at the red paving found along the streets of Frontierland in the Magic Kingdom of Walt Disney World. Shortly before the opening of Walt Disney World in 1971, Marketing Director Jack Lindquist was asked to fly to Boston. Workers were ready to pour concrete for the red-colored pavings throughout the Magic Kingdom, but there was no red coloring powder. It was Friday. And it needed to be available by Monday morning. No problem. Jack spent his weekend on a rescue mission to Boston, chartering a plane, obtaining the colored powder, and arriving just in time for construction work on Monday.

It was that kind of an "all hands on deck" attitude that made Walt Disney World a reality. Jack Lindquist knew that, and he extended a hand whenever called upon. In time, he would come to be president of the Disneyland Resort in California.

That same sensibility continues today at Disney in what is known as Cross-U. One of the traditions at the Disney parks is that of utilizing office and "heart of the house" Cast Members out in the parks during peak holiday seasons. It's called Cross-U (for Utilization), and it offers many advantages:

1. It supports the "heavy lifting" that front line Cast Members must carry when there are throngs of Guests out in the parks.

2. It gives those who don't work with the Guests an opportunity to better appreciate what front line Cast Members have to do.

3. It saves the company money on the bottom line by not having to employ so many seasonal workers.

4. Most importantly, it helps support the Guest experience by having more Cast Members available to help answer questions and direct the experience of the Guests.

As a Cast Member, I thought Cross-U was fantastic. My formal office with The Disney Institute was miles away closer to Sea World than Walt Disney World. Some of my favorite memories were out in the parks, working counter service areas or helping out with the parade. I valued the experience and gained greater insight into the entire operation at Walt Disney World.

Of course, from time to time some office Cast Members resented having to do Cross-U, arguing that they had "better things" to attend to. Some see it as "beneath them." Others view the request as some form of indentured servitude or that Disney is simply trying to trim the budget when they can get away with it. **Even Disney Cast Members need to understand that the real magic comes to them when they make the sacrifice to go**

out to serve—even when it means working with less.
That view comes in clearly in this next example.

An Outrageous Fortune Making Do With Less
LEADERS DON'T EQUATE EXCELLENCE WITH HAVING
A BIG BUDGET

No one likes hearing the expression "making do with less." The
effect can be demoralizing, and you wonder when, or if, things are
turning a corner for the worst. But the truth is, "making do with
less" is a reality even for the "Happiest Place on Earth." It's been
around the Walt Disney Company for as long as there has been a
Walt Disney Company. Between fantastic hits like *Snow White and
the Seven Dwarfs* and *Mary Poppins* and *Star Wars: The Force Awakens*
were lean, difficult times where the budget was hacked and people
had to "make do with less."

Such a time came about not long after Michael Eisner came
aboard the company. That's when a certain screenwriter named
Leslie Dixon was hired. In the 1980s and into the 1990s, Dixon
became somewhat of a poster child for "making do with less." She
is a screenwriter and was the granddaughter of landscape painter
Maynard Dixon and photographer Dorothea Lange (you'll
perhaps recall Lange's work reflected in Disney's California
Adventure attraction, Golden Dreams, where the migrant woman
is having her picture taken along with her children during the
Great Depression). Given that parental legacy however, didn't
mean opportunity would come on a golden platter. Dixon would
pay her dues like any other, particularly in getting her break into
show business.

Her first solo opportunity was to write the screenplay for the 1987
film, *Outrageous Fortune*. That film starred Bette Midler and Shelley
Long; that is, assuming you were east of the Mississippi. If you
were west of the Mississippi, it starred Shelley Long and Bette
Midler in that order. Neither would concede on top billing, hence
the compromise as to who would receive top billing was divided

geographically.

There is a scene toward the beginning of the film where Shelley Long was going to approach her parents about borrowing $5,000 so she could study with the great theater professor, Stanislav Korzenowski. Dixon's script called for the scene to take place in the parents' apartment, where Long would plead with her parents. In trying to cut back on the film's budget, it was determined that it was not worth the cost of building a set like that for such a small scene. Dixon was asked to go back and rewrite the scene some other way so that it could be filmed for less money.

Dixon resented having to do the rewrite. The rewritten scene occurred on the street in front of the parents' apartment complex and actually was quite funny, because of how the location was changed. It certainly shows Dixon's resourcefulness in doing more with less. In fact, the scene is probably better than what it would have been if it had been filmed with a bigger budget using the apartment as the backdrop.

That's not to say that she liked doing it. She found Disney to be a real tightwad, and frankly, a pain to deal with. But Leslie conceded that **the pain of doing more with less forces one's self to be more creative than one would have been otherwise.** In the end, the film was a box-office hit. To date, it has grossed domestically some $53 million, not a lot in today's terms, but not bad for a film that was created for a fraction of its return. Dixon was under contract to write another screenplay for Disney. She resisted taking on the assignment, but she eventually gave into the contract to do the movie *Big Business*, which also was a hit for Disney at the time.

In Michael Eisner's memoir, *Work in Progress*, he noted in the years to follow that Dixon was in high demand throughout Hollywood. Conversely, Dixon vowed she would never work for Disney again. Indeed, she compared her experience at Disney to indentured servitude. She left to go write comedies for other studios. Her success there did not come so easily. In the end, she came to realize that maybe all of the stinginess she found at Disney was not as unreasonable as it initially seemed. She stated:

> Was [working for Disney] a good experience for me? No.
> If I were them, would I have done the same thing?
> Probably. Would I write for them again? Well, let me just
> say that time and wisdom have made me miss their
> marketing department with every fiber of my body.

Leslie Dixon would eventually go on to provide the screenplays of some great films, like *Mrs. Doubtfire*, *Hairspray*, *Pay it Forward*, and even Disney's remake of *Freaky Friday*. In the years to come Disney would forget the lessons of being resourceful, creating a number of big budget films. Some of those would reap huge returns like *Pirates of the Caribbean: The Curse of the Black Pearl*. Others like *Pearl Harbor* and *John Carter* would be disappointments at the box office.

Such was the case when, a few years after *Outrageous Fortune*, Disney released a very expensive film called *Dick Tracy*. Starring Warren Beatty, this comic strip film was expected to be a Disney hit. Disney was disappointed in the end with the results, compared to *Batman* with Michael Keaton, which was a runaway hit the year previous.

Regarding this period, Jeffrey Katzenberg expressed disappointment when he said, "We made demands on our time, talent, and treasury that, upon reflection, may not have been worth it."

Of this, Eisner made note in his memoirs:

> Our initial success at Disney was based on the ability to
> sell good stories well. Big stars, special effects and name
> directors were of little importance. Of course, we started
> this way out of necessity. We had small budgets and not
> much respect. So we substituted dollars with creativity and
> big stars with talent we believed in. Success ensued. With
> success came bigger budgets and bigger names. We found
> ourselves attracting the caliber of talent with which
> "event" monies could be made. And more and more we
> began making them. The result: costs have escalated,

profitability has slipped and our level of risk has compounded. The time has come to get back to our roots.

Pink Elephants of Success
LEADERS FIND EFFICIENT WAYS TO CREATE EXCELLENCE

The roots, however, are in Walt Disney, who himself learned about how to manage the bad times as well as the good. He, of course, wanted quality, as do most people. He certainly achieved that with a film like *Snow White and the Seven Dwarfs*, which was coincidentally re-released at the same time as *Outrageous Fortune*, yet still managed to bring in $45 million from just that release. But Walt Disney also experienced the reality that spending money alone did not a successful picture make. He reasoned that if *Snow White* was an artistic achievement, then *Pinocchio*, which followed, should be an even greater artistic effort. But all the beauty and artistry (and the costs associated) didn't save *Pinocchio* in the box office. So they took a different approach on their next film. Making do with less, they released *Dumbo*, which would only cost Walt one-third of *Pinocchio*'s cost to produce, yet it grossed more in theaters.

Walt experienced the same effect with *Sleeping Beauty*, which tanked at the time after a very laborious effort to bring it to life. *Sleeping Beauty* is an exquisite film. It's practically an artistic canvas brought to life. But audiences didn't care that much when it was finally released, not really empathizing with the dormant princess. Sometimes doing more with less means getting to the heart of what really matters—in this case it was story and character.

Sleeping Beauty was followed by *101 Dalmatians*, which was far more successful in the box office, as well as profitable. Getting back to the basics, they focused on story and character. But in order to do more with less, technicians thought out of the box by utilizing a new technology that would save time in clean up and inking— especially with all of those little Dalmatian spots! We know that invention in its current form today as the Xerox machine.

At the end of the day, it's about quality...and about being creative around making do with less. It's simply how you approach those ventures creatively that makes the magic in your business. Of course, sometimes being too resourceful can also come back to haunt you, as we learn from Fort Wilderness's own heritage at Walt Disney World.

Kambak's Raiders
LEADERS PROVIDE OTHERS WITH THE RESOURCES THEY NEED

Legend and lore has it that somewhere during the construction of Walt Disney World, Card Walker called Dick Nunis one day and asked him how the Florida project was going. Nunis replied that it was moving on schedule, but it was struggling from going over budget. Walker then asked how the campgrounds were coming along. Nunis said "What campground?" Walker then reminded Nunis of Walt's vision that Walt Disney World would offer accommodations for every kind of Guest, from "a sleeping bag to a suite." Walt Disney World simply had to open with a campground.

The story goes that Nunis then called up Keith Kambak, who was initially responsible for the marina/pools/recreation part of the Walt Disney World complex. Nunis asked Kambak how the campground was coming along. Kambak replied, "What campground?" Nunis then reminded Kambak of Walt Disney's vision that there would be accommodations from sleeping bags to suites, and charged Keith with getting the campground open.

Such was the birth of the Fort Wilderness campground. It began almost as an afterthought and would continue for many years in the shadows of everything else, with little assigned budget. To that end, Kambak formed a team known as "Kambak's Raiders." For instance, a shovel was just a shovel anywhere at Walt Disney World. But moved to Fort Wilderness from another end of the property and painted green (Fort Wilderness's color marking), suddenly it was a Fort Wilderness asset. It wasn't the ideal way to acquire the resources you needed, but sometimes you had to go underground to get the work done (even if you couldn't dig underground in a swamp).

Perhaps this ultimately didn't play out in Fort Wilderness's favor. For instance, under this organizational structure, they had access to the pontoon boats. And with those boats, they could float over to Pluto's Park to look around for materials that would help them improve Fort Wilderness. Pluto's Park is also known as the bone yard (Pluto burying bones) and is more of a final resting place for stuff that has no place to go. For instance, for many years it was where the 20,000 Leagues Under the Sea submarines were kept after they were taken from the lagoon. But in the earlier years, it was where construction materials were kept until they were needed on site. Its location is on the opposite end of Bay Lake from Fort Wilderness, making it ideal to access from pontoon boats. It was here that Kambak's Raiders late at night found pallets of railroad ties—perfect for lining sidewalks that were originally made of coquina, a mixture of mineral and crushed shell found throughout Florida. It provided a more stable foundation than dirt and sand when it came to paving. It was also more affordable than asphalt, for which there was no money. The downside was that the coquina would scatter and kill the grass, which wasn't good show. Therefore, these railroad ties laying around in Pluto's Park would be perfect for lining the sidewalks so that the coquina wouldn't spill over.

So beam-by-beam, materials were soon transported late at night by Kambak's Raiders. Over time, some really nice looking sidewalks lined with beams emerged. There was just one downside. Unbeknownst to Kambak's Raiders, corporate had decided to fix the challenges that were occurring on the Fort Wilderness Railroad, which ran throughout the campground. In order to fix those problems, they had contracted with Georgia Pacific, who would come down and improve the rail line so that it wouldn't derail. The pallets of railroad ties were now missing and Georgia Pacific was irate that they couldn't get the job done. When corporate couldn't explain what happened to the beams, things started falling apart. In time, focus and budget on the train went to other Walt Disney World projects.

Such was the demise of the Fort Wilderness Railroad. But it is a learning experience that ultimately, you need to support your staff with the resources they need in order for them to be successful. **Having workers go "underground" in order to get the job done is not a recipe for being resourceful.**

The Backside of Water—With a Flair
LEADERS ADD AN EXTRA TOUCH

A highlight of the world-famous Jungle Cruise is the opportunity to visit "the backside of water". To Disney fans, and especially Jungle Cruise enthusiasts, the expression "The Backside of Water" holds a very unique image in their minds. **Sometimes when it comes to going the extra mile, it can be the simplest, most economical effort that makes all the difference in the world.**

Schweitzer Falls has seemingly been a focal point of the Jungle Cruise since it was constructed in 1955. It began as a nod to African missionary Dr. Albert Schweitzer, or as many a Jungle Cruise skipper has poked fun, "a tribute to Dr. Albert Falls." The Jungle Cruise was one of the signature attractions on opening day. It was important that the attraction be as exciting and dramatic as possible. The waterfall in many ways was a focal point, first seen as your boat swings around to avoid it, and then again later as your boat sails behind it. The sensation of going behind the falls has been a nearly tangible, tactile experience.

It's since been repeated in the Jungle Cruise at the Magic Kingdom at Walt Disney World, and at Tokyo Disneyland. So iconic has Schweitzer Falls become that Dr. Falls himself was attached to the name of the signature steak at the Skipper Canteen at the Magic Kingdom. Is there really a difference between any grilled steak and a Dr. Falls Signature Grilled Steak? Not really. But the title gives the menu choice a little flair. Just like the falls.

But what does giving something a little flair really mean? On the 10th anniversary of Disneyland, Walt spoke to Cast Members assembled for a celebration given at the Disneyland Hotel. To the audience, he spoke about the early days, and the challenges of getting everything started:

> A lot of people don't realize we had some very serious problems here, keeping this thing going ... getting it started. I remember when we opened we didn't have enough money to finish the landscaping. I had Bill Evans [original head of landscaping] go and put Latin tags on all of the weeds. We had a lot of inquiries. That's a fact. You ask Bill Evans. Of course, every weed to Bill Evans has got a Latin name, you know.

During the opening of Disneyland, even the weeds were given a little flair to make them interesting. It sort of reminds me of the lyrics to a Sherman Brothers' *Bedknobs and Broomsticks* tune, "With a Flair":

> *Oh, it really doesn't matter what I do, what I do*
> *As long as I do it with a flair*
> *What effect a little smoke is with a dash of hocus pocus*
> *And the scent of burning sulfur in the air*
>
> *I'm a fraud, a hoke, a charlatan, a joke,*
> *But they love me ... everywhere.*
> *For it really doesn't matter what I do, what I do*
> *As long as I do it with a flair*

In truth, Walt was no charlatan. The popularity and endurance of Disneyland decades later bears testimony to that. Disneyland's legacy was not born in a day. Those early years were difficult. And while he put everything financially on the line to make Disneyland a reality, it still had its shortcomings. It would be years before it would be perfected to the state it is today. **When you don't have the budget you want, it's still important to give anything and everything a little flair.**

Walt Disney would also go on to say about those early weeds:

> I wanted something live, something that could grow,
> something I could keep plussing with ideas, you see?
> The park is that. Not only can I add things but even the
> trees will keep growing; the thing will get more beautiful
> every year.

A dedication to excellence? Yes. And over time it's about
perfecting and plussing, as we'll discuss in the next couple of
chapters. But to get it started, it sometimes begins with just a little
flair.

Leadership & You

As a leader, consider the following:

- What does "Green Side Up" look like in my organization?

- What does "Naming the Sheriff" look like in my organization?

- How do I cultivate a culture of helping to pitch in even when
  doing something that isn't necessarily my job requirement?

- How do I celebrate those who go the extra mile beyond their
  regular duties?

- What are the benefits of cross-utilizing my employees?

- Am I being asked to make do with less? Do I resist having to
  do so?

- Do I feel that the only way to succeed is by investing as much
  money and time as possible?

- Are there creative ways to make do with less?

- Do some in my organization have an attitude that "it's not my
  job"? How do I ultimately get people focused on doing what

really matters, and not doing just what their job description provides?

- How do I support my team with the resources my employees need?

- What do I do to keep employees from having to go "underground" to get the job done?

- What is the "backside of water" in my own business?

- How can I take even the weeds of my business and plus them?

- What is the extra touch I can bring to what is otherwise unexpected?

- How can I give a flair even to those products and services that still aren't perfect?

7

PUT YOUR BEHIND IN YOUR PAST
LEADERS LEARN FROM THEIR MISTAKES

Pumbaa: It's like my buddy Timon always says, "You got to put your behind in your past."

Timon: No, no, no. Amateur. Sit down before you hurt yourself. It's "You got to put your past behind you."

Either way gets the point across, but perhaps Rafiki summed it up better when he counseled Simba, "Oh yes, the past can hurt. But from the way I see it, you can either run from it or learn from it."

Like Simba in *The Lion King*, leaders make mistakes. Everyone makes mistakes. As a leader, your efforts should not center on mistakes, but on gathering the experience necessary to be successful in the long run. The passages in this chapter look at some key lessons around this. It begins with an attitude toward learning.

The Black Hole of "Why Bother"
LEADERS KEEP PROGRESSING

While it looks like winter on Matterhorn Mountain year round, there's no time of the year more beautiful than the holiday season at Disneyland. For years, Christmas decorations have graced Disneyland and, at one time, a large star stood at the top of the Matterhorn. It even lit up and rotated.

Unfortunately for Disney's Cast Members, the month of

December has not always been a happy time. It was during the holiday season of 1966 when the Cast learned that Walt Disney had passed away unexpectedly. In their shock, several managers, including Van France, sought refuge at a lounge located at the Disneyland Hotel. There, they shared remembrances for several hours.

Van recalls the experience in his own work, *Windows on Main Street*. As they got ready to leave, one member of management turned to the other and mentioned that the star on top of the Matterhorn had broken again. The other manager shrugged it off, as if to say, "Why bother?" At that moment, his colleague turned to him and said, "You wouldn't shrug it off if Walt were here."

A few years later, the star was removed but the conversation marked the beginning of a dialogue that has continued to this day, with Cast Members asking, **"What would Walt do?"** That philosophy carried the organization forward for many years. In part, it worked because Walt had laid down key principles about how to run the park. Partly out of loyalty, and partly out of habit, Cast Members referred to those ideals.

Still, one of Walt's most tenured animators, Ward Kimball, noted that if you were instinctively in tune, you wouldn't have to ask the question. He himself had learned excellence intuitively. Ward learned that excellence, as Walt had taught, was not in repeating one's self, or in going back in time to consider what others would do, but in moving forward and in bringing new ideas to the table. After all, he reasoned, that is just exactly what Walt would have done.

Unfortunately, after Walt's, and especially after Roy O. Disney's, passing a few years later, those leading Walt Disney Productions at that time were not following that mantra. I personally remember being given the opportunity to tour the studio in the summer of 1978. I couldn't have been more excited about this experience—to me, it was the equivalent of going into Willy Wonka's chocolate factory. I had seen photos, but nothing quite prepared me for this. We were ushered into a small waiting area with faded wood paneling and missing ceiling tiles.

Our first stop was a junkyard of the parts belonging to Herbie the Love Bug. I loved Herbie, but the series, having done three films, had already started to fade. Parts were left in anticipation of doing a fourth film in the series, which would become known as *Herbie Goes Bananas*. It was fascinating and sad at the same time.

We toured the animation studios. What struck me was that there didn't seem to be anybody working. We walked the tunnel over to Ink and Paint. No one was there either. It was summer, but it was awfully quiet—even retired.

We toured the backlot, to include sets from *Zorro* and other films from the past. We would have toured the sound stages but there was a top-secret film being created and no one other than cast and crew were permitted inside. It turns out the film would be known as *The Black Hole*. The film sounded promising, but in truth, it was really an effort to eat the crumbs from the table of *Star Wars*. Management missed the opportunity to do that film with George Lucas, and now it was trying to make up for it by doing a similar film. Clearly the studio stood rudderless.

It was no surprise that the ground shook when Michael Eisner and Frank Wells came aboard a few years later. Under Michael and Frank, business as usual gave way to serious change. In their wake, every part of the company was expected to move forward. In his words, Michael stated, **"Standing still was not an option. Either you take calculated risks to grow, or you slowly wither and die."** With that, the Studio made major changes, which ultimately led to a new renaissance of creativity and productivity.

Looking at your own life, do you have the courage not to conform, or not stick with the status quo? Does that courage make you dream of something better, something greater? You can't afford to become stale. Nor can you afford to shy away from taking risks. Risk taking is pivotal to successful organizations. That includes Disney.

Sinking the Mark Twain
LEADERS CREATE A LEARNING CULTURE

Another important principle for moving forward is to create a culture that allows people to learn from their mistakes.

The Mark Twain opened to the general public at Disneyland on July 17th, 1955. Walt loved the beautiful ships that would sail down the mighty Mississippi. They were elegant, but fragile. With all of its intricate lattice, one had to be careful not to ground her on the riverbed (hence the depth calls of "Mark One" and "Mark Twain"). One also had to be careful of boilers overheating, blowing up, and resulting in a fatal calamity.

By the time this replica of a steamboat opened, those sorts of concerns had long been resolved. But there were still other problems to be encountered. Cast Member Terry O'Brien was one of the first Cast Members hired at that time. While observing all of the excitement of that opening day with its parades and celebrities, like Art Linkletter and Ronald Reagan, it was easy to be distracted.

O'Brien's role was to admit Guests into the holding area where they would await the next ship. Since the ship was brand new, they really had no idea how many to admit at one time onto the ship. The designers estimated the number should be kept around 200-300. With no turnstile, Terry was given a clicker, and all day he would click as people entered into the holding area.

After a while, the job became mundane, so O'Brien started chatting with Guests. The ship came into the landing and another group took off. Shortly afterwards, the ship signaled trouble. With so many Guests on board, the boat had derailed off the track and sunk into the mud. It took a while for management to get it fixed and back on the rail. As it came back to the landing, all the people rushed to the side to get off, and the boat tipped into the water again.

The supervisor approached Terry O'Brien and asked how many people he'd put on the boat. Quickly, Terry responded "about 250," to which the supervisor suggested that it stay at around 200. As the supervisor left, Terry took a look at the clicker and realized that he had actually put 508 passengers aboard the Mark Twain. Embarrassed, he told no one. Terry made sure that it never happened again.

The reality is that everyone makes mistakes and we must create a learning culture so that people learn from those mistakes. When we don't allow people to make mistakes and learn from those mistakes, they tend to go underground. Much preferred is an organization that permits people to identify lessons from their mistakes and to use them as opportunities for improving the organization.

You might think this earlier story runs counter to what "carnival experts" told Walt Disney when they warned him that he needed the "carnies" to run the parks. But Walt countered that philosophy: "In the first place," said Walt, "this is not an amusement park. In the second place, we can run Disneyland as well as anyone. Walt then stated: **"All you need are people who are eager, energetic, friendly, and willing to learn. They'll make mistakes, but we can learn from their mistakes."**

Figaro's Mistake
LEADERS CELEBRATE LESSONS LEARNED

When Disneyland opened, there was no attraction or experience based on the journeys of Pinocchio. So with the creation of the Magic Kingdom at Walt Disney World, Imagineers developed a counter-service restaurant concept based on Walt Disney's second full-length feature film.

Known as Pinocchio's Village Haus, this very large fast food facility is broken into smaller rooms, each themed to one of

Pinocchio's companions. One of them includes Figaro the cat.

When Disneyland redeveloped Fantasyland in 1983, Imagineers sought to finally create an attraction based on the film. But they also brought the same successful food and beverage concept over as well. There was only one problem: When installing the exit sign, something got messed up along the way and the fixture ended up being off-center from the doorway.

While it still functioned appropriately as an emergency exit sign, it simply looked silly. No problem. Imagineers painted Figaro tugging on the exit sign. Suddenly it seemed like it fit just fine.

But Imagineers didn't stop there. When they built the same style restaurant in Disneyland Paris, they remembered to get that exit sign right. And in celebrating that lesson learned, they painted Figaro giving a big thumbs up. In Disney-speak, that's a sign for "good show".

The message is about learning from one's mistakes and moving forward (indeed, that is the central message in *Pinocchio*). Better yet, let's celebrate and learn from those mistakes.

ABC's Wide World of Learning
LEADERS OWN UP TO THEIR MISTAKES

Consider Bob Iger's own experience years prior during his sportscasting career:

> **Early on, I learned that if you owned your own failure, or embraced whatever disappointment, it was probably the best way to process and overcome the failure and disappointment.** I remember early in my ABC Sports days a relatively trivial mistake had been made on a weekend sporting event on Wide World of Sports, where we simply missed a story that we should have had. In a Monday-morning session that the former head of ABC Sports Roone Arledge held,

which was typically a postmortem of what went on during the weekend, whatever we had missed came up. There was silence around the room as Roone questioned what happened. At the time, I was young and low-titled and said, "It was my mistake. I missed that." There was complete silence in the room. Everyone looked around. Here, I had admitted in front of the brass of then-ABC Sports, including the head of it, that I had made a mistake.

It was the most empowering thing I could have ever done. We moved on. But what was interesting to me about this was that it was a lesson. It was probably the first time I ever owned up to something like that in such a way. Looking back, it was relatively trivial, but it was unbelievably empowering. And the respect that people had for me doing that actually put me in a stronger, better position with everybody.

It taught me that if you failed, you have an ability to not just accept the failure and attempt to understand it but to be accountable [Owning up to failure] offers the best chance to recover from it. It's a lesson I've taken with me throughout [my career]. If something fails as a direct result of your decision and you take responsibility for it, you're much more likely to endure than if you do the opposite.

Can you imagine the outcome for ABC—for all of The Walt Disney Company—if Iger had been canned for making that mistake? If you want a company that exceeds, you must take risks. And you can't have a risk-taking organization if you don't have a learning organization. And you can't learn without making mistakes.

The Good Lesson From The Good Dinosaur
LEADERS LEARN FROM REAL FAILURE

It takes risk to make movies. No one has known this any more than Pixar. It has taken huge risks and has had hit after hit. Their films have been juggernauts at the box office and critically acclaimed. *Toy Story, Monsters Inc., Finding Nemo, The Incredibles*. The list goes on and on.

But what Pixar hadn't really known was failure.

Then came *The Good Dinosaur*. Oh, it was good. It has even had some solid initial sales as it has entered the home video sales arena. But the box office itself wasn't great. And good is not great at Pixar.

Still, that's okay–according to Ed Catmull, Pixar's pioneering leader. Here's what he's had to say in his book, *Creativity Inc.*, about risk and failure:

- "Failure isn't a necessary evil. In fact, it isn't evil at all; it is a necessary consequence of doing something new."

- "It's not the leader/manager's job to prevent risks. It's the leader/manager's job to make sure it is safe for others to take them."

- "Trust doesn't mean that you trust someone won't screw up— it means you trust them even when they do screw up."

- "The desire for everything to run smoothly is a false goal—it leads to measuring people by their mistakes they make rather than by their ability to solve problems."

If you expect real performance, expect real failure. The two go hand in hand. If Pixar has created a culture that embraces both risk and failure, it will do great learning from the experience and moving forward.

What Pixar does know is to learn from its mistakes. Well into production of *Toy Story 2*, someone accidentally gave a command to the Unix and Linux machines used to store the thousands of computer files that comprise the shots of the entire film. That command completely erased 90 percent of the film in a matter of seconds. First Woody disappeared, then Buzz. Mr. Potato Head, Hamm, and Rex quickly followed. Entire sequences were suddenly deleted from the drive.

Of course, Pixar knew that you needed to keep up a backup system. The answer was to restore the date from those computers. Only a half day of work would be lost. But then came the realization that the backup system hadn't been working correctly. *Toy Story 2* was now completely deleted. To reassemble the film would require thirty people working for a solid year.

In what was a miracle, it came to the organization's attention that the technical director of the film had been making backups on her home computer. She had a baby six months prior, and in trying to spend more time at home, she had set up a system that copied the film's database to her home computer automatically once a week. As Ed Catmull relates in his book, they ran back to the house, wrapped the computer in blankets, drove in the slow lane all the way back to the office, and then "carried the computer carefully into Pixar like an Egyptian pharaoh."

Serendipitous? Perhaps. But luck can still favor you when misfortune doesn't. Did they learn from that lesson? Yes. They not only restored the film, but they fixed their backup systems and installed precautionary restrictions to make it more difficult to access the deletion command directly.

But Ed Catmull then counters:

> **Notably one item was *not* on our list: Find the person responsible who typed the wrong command and punish him or her.** Some people may question that decision, reasoning that as valuable as creating a trusting environment can be, responsibility without accountability can undermine an expectation of excellence. I'm all for accountability. But in this case, my reasoning went like this: Our people have good intentions. To think you can control or prevent random problems by making an example of someone is naïve and wrongheaded. (italics added)

Leadership & You

As a leader, consider the following:

- Is my organization a learning culture?

- Do I allow people to learn from their mistakes, or do I hold it against them?

- What can I do to send a message that we should not only learn from our mistakes, but also share them to the benefit of others?

- Am I taking risks?

- Am I experiencing failure? If the answer is no to the latter, you may not be taking big enough risks. Risk and failure go hand in hand.

8

PRACTICALLY PERFECT IN EVERY WAY
LEADERS SEEK EXCELLENCE

"Practically perfect in every way" exquisitely sums up the magic that is Mary Poppins. It also sums up the cinematic work itself, which was a tally of everything Walt Disney had pioneered and fine-tuned in animation and film. Notably that pinnacle day in his career occurred near the end of it, after decades of working hard to hone and refine his craft. Such is excellence. It is not a state of arrival, but instead an unending process.

There were three things that supported Walt in perfecting his work. Let's take a look at them.

Mickey Mouse Improvements
LEADERS MAKE IMPROVEMENTS ALONG THE WAY

What made Mickey Mouse initially successful was not that he was the first animated character ever, because animation had been going on for some time. Rather, Walt took the medium to the next level by showcasing the mouse as a talking animated short. Talking pictures were new, and Mickey was first animated character on the scene to provide that sort of experience to theatergoers.

Walt built on that lesson by continually refining his craft. The *Silly Symphonies* were opportunities for Walt to explore new technologies in the medium. The use of Technicolor and the invention of the multi-plane camera were outcomes of that effort.

But Walt also wanted the images on the screen to improve. As he embarked on building his first full-length animated film, *Snow White and the Seven Dwarfs*, he knew that his artists needed to refine their skills in drawing humans realistically. So he sent them off to school. As early as 1931, Walt was paying for artists to attend evening classes at Chouinard Art Institute in Los Angeles. The following year, Walt invited Donald Graham to start an art-training program at the Hyperion studio, with the goal of recruiting no fewer than 300 new artists. In my book, *Disney's Hollywood Studios: From Show Biz to Your Biz*, I note that Graham had recalled:

> From eight in the morning till nine at night, what was probably the most unique art school in the world was conducted. As *Snow White* began to take shape, various experts from all branches of the studio were called upon to contribute to the program. Intensive lectures on character construction, animation, layout, background, mechanics, and direction extended studio knowledge to the youngest neophyte.

Walt knew that to be better than what others were doing he had to perfect his organization's technical as well as artistic craft. Investing in technology started from the beginning. Continuous learning and development is vital as well.

You Can't Top Pigs with Pigs
Leaders Don't Repeat Themselves

Walt's creation of the *Silly Symphonies* was due, in part, to the fact that Mickey shorts were artistically limiting. The *Silly Symphonies* offered opportunities to create variety. *The Three Little Pigs*, one of the most popular, was so well received that the distributor wanted more Little Pigs shorts. Walt's concern was that they were just topping pigs with pigs. He stated: "You hate to repeat yourself. I don't like to make sequels to my pictures. I like to take a new thing and develop something, a new concept."

Snow White and the Seven Dwarfs, the *True-Life Adventures* series, his debut into television, Disneyland, and the notion for building EPCOT were all examples of developing new ideas and concepts. It continued throughout his life. **Simply put: In the quest for excellence, leaders can't be formulaic.** They have to create new concepts and ideas. To that end, the *Pirates of the Caribbean* films broke ground by offering something new in that genre that hadn't been successful in the box office for decades. Yet, the studio has to learn that simply topping pirates with pirates is not enough.

Fish & Chips
LEADERS CREATE FOR CONTINUOUS IMPROVEMENT

Continuous improvement is an important part of perfecting an organization. Great organizations succeed when employees give input to new ideas. Implementing excellence must be the work of all employees. This was played out with Cast Members at the Rose & Crown, a sit down restaurant at Epcot. The restaurant was introduced to a continuous improvement cycle and, as a team, they discussed what implications there were in this type of process. When Cast Members were empowered to identify opportunities to improve service, they delivered; they noticed that people were asking if there was a place they could order fish and chips "to go". It's offered on the menu at this restaurant, but there was no counter service offering.

Cast Members began to tally the number of times such responses were being heard. The end result was that there was a demand for fish and chips. One's initial response might be to simply petition management for a counter service restaurant to address the solution. But rather than creating a new food outlet, they began testing the interest in fish and chips by offering it to go at the pub. Those who expressed interest in fish & chips "to go" were sent to a space created for that purpose at the corner of the bar. They then measured the results of that effort.

The interest over the months to follow was so positive that they tested it further by opening a temporary set up outside of the restaurant. Of course, Disney doesn't do "lemonade stands" on the fly, but they did have a number of resources they could pull together to create a nice, though temporary, facility. The location was fairly ideal since it allowed them to run food out of the back door of the kitchen.

The success of the kiosk was measured over time. In fact, it ran long enough so that they could test whether interest was just a fad, or whether there was long term interest. They also measured its effect on other food and beverage facilities found in adjoining properties.

The end result of this continuous improvement effort was successful, and as a result, you now see a formal, outdoor counter service location known as Yorkshire County Fish Shop. During most times of the day, you'll usually find someone lined up to sample these British morsels.

This is a sample of what is replicated not only at Epcot, but all over Walt Disney World. **Employee engagement works best when Disney invites its Cast Members to find new ways to improve.** Not only does it make the Guest experience better, but inviting the frontline employees to participate in the overall success of an operation engages your workers.

In their efforts to improve your organization, leaders need to identify a system for tracking and monitoring progress on an ongoing basis. And when you do, what is the result? A workforce that is more engaged, more involved, and more active in wanting to create excellence throughout the entire organization. And…one that creates winning results!

Jiro Dreams of Sushi
LEADERS SEEK PERFECTION

Walt Disney Company CEO Bob Iger has delivered big results, especially in seeking to bring aboard Pixar, Marvel, Lucasfilm, and Fox. He has also opened a major Disney resort in Mainland China. But what captures Bob's interest was shown when, in an interview with *Variety* on being named Showman of the Year, he chose to acknowledge his own fascination with the work of Jiro Ono, who at the age of 91, has the reputation of being the world's greatest sushi chef.

Jiro, who is the focus of the documentary *Jiro Dreams of Sushi*, has a modest 10-seat sushi bar in a Tokyo subway station, and yet it has achieved Michelin three-star status.

The documentary—so titled because Jiro would dream of sushi at night, jumping out of his bed with new ideas—shares some important messages from Jiro's life:

> **Once you decide on your occupation, you must immerse yourself in your work. You have to fall in love with your work. Never complain about your job. You must dedicate your life to mastering your skill. That is the secret to success.**
>
> All I want to do is to make better sushi. I do the same thing over and over, improving it bit by bit. There is always a yearning to achieve more. I'll continue to climb, trying to reach the top, but no one knows where the top is.
>
> I've never once hated this job, and gave my life to it…Even at my age, after decades of work, I don't think I have achieved perfection.

Consider the examples of Jiro Ono's drive for self-improvement. For instance, it was easier for him in the early years to boil the shrimp in the morning, put it in the fridge, and then serve later. But now he boils it at the time he makes the sushi, and while that's more effort, it makes a better dish. The same could be said of the octopus, which he massages 40-50 minutes, rather than 30 minutes as he did in the past.

All of these messages were so impactful that Bob Iger hosted an offsite with his management team emphasizing the messages Jiro brings. Clearly, Bob links this epiphany to his work over the last number of years. But what must happen is not just that the message be spread to the senior management team. It's critical that every Cast Member at Disney embrace these same ideas.

How can tens of thousands of Cast Members working in a massive operation like Disney embrace these ideals? The answer is, one person at a time. One team at a time. It's not something that can be "mandated" or "hard wired" from above. Rather, management must create the strategy, and then turn the organization pyramid upside down, and ask themselves, "How can we support the Cast in their efforts to deliver and perfect their labors?" Leadership is more about how you inspire and motivate others to be their best, rather than mandating some program.

The Opportunity for Any Organization
LEADERS MAKE EXCELLENCE A HABIT, NOT AN ACT

I see this in my own work with other organizations. Management sees the need for change–for improvement. So what do they do? They reorganize. And yet, what does it create? American Journalist Charlton Ogburn once summarized the Burma Campaign in World War II as follows:

> We trained hard, but it seemed that every time we were beginning to form up into teams we would be reorganized. Presumably the plans for our employment were being changed. **I was to learn later in life that, perhaps because we are so good at organizing, we tend as a nation to meet any new situation by reorganizing; and a wonderful method it can be for creating the illusion of progress while producing confusion, inefficiency, and demoralization.** During our reorganizations, several commanding officers were tried out on us, which added to the discontinuity.

Others spend millions on new technology hoping for advances, yet often its promises come up short. The reality is, even though there is a time and place for investing in technology—or even to reorganize, those efforts will seldom succeed if there is not a culture that empowers employees to succeed. Creating an environment that allows thousands of Jiros to succeed is what is needed.

It is in the spirit of Jiro that we see the possibilities of what an organization can be—each individual working to constantly be their very best—finding new ways to improve daily. As Will Durrant summed up in his study of Aristotle's *Nicomachean Ethics*, "We are what we repeatedly do. Excellence, then, is not an act, but a habit."

That is how Disney, or any entity, can become the greatest organization in the world—every employee obsessed with excellence—not just the CEO. That quest is at the doorstop of every organization seeking excellence.

Leadership & You

As a leader, consider the following:

- How am I pushing the envelope for excellence?

- How am I supporting my staff in being better today than they were yesterday?

- What continuous improvement processes do I have in my organization?

- What opportunities exist for improving my organization?

- How do I push organizational improvement to the front line?

- How would employees be more engaged with this kind of process?

SECTION
III

LEADERS BUILD
RELATIONSHIPS

"I have an organization of people who are really specialists. You can't match them anywhere in the world for what they can do. But they all need to be pulled together. We have set up a plan of working together and helping each other. They're not afraid to admit that they're licked on a certain problem and try to get the help from someone else."

--Walt Disney

9

IT TAKES PEOPLE
TO MAKE THE DREAM A REALITY
LEADERS BUILD MORALE

The full quote is this:

"You can design and create, and build the most wonderful place in the world. But it takes people to make the dream a reality."
　　—Walt Disney

These words are located on a window on Main Street, U.S.A. at both Disneyland and Walt Disney World. At Disneyland, they are accompanied by a playful jobs ad which lists varying fictional positions, like Tahitian dancers, a pirate crew, mermaids, and even one airborne pixie. They all reference the different positions that exist in the Magic Kingdom parks. All of those roles are important to the Guest experience. And all those jobs require an engaged workforce led by leaders that build the morale of Cast Members.

6 out of 7 Dwarfs are NOT Happy
LEADERS FOCUS ON MORALE

So true. It's also true that 6 out of 7 dwarfs are NOT Grumpy. With all of the Disney blogs out there, you will hear of both very happy and very grumpy employees. But in general, how satisfied are Disney employees? What is the morale?

I speak largely to those ideas in our book, *Lead With Your Customer: Transform Culture and Brand into World-Class Excellence*; the premise being that it's really two sides of the same coin, and that to be effective with external customers, you have to be effective with internal customers. So it's important that we focus on engaging employees and raising morale.

Brad Bird, Oscar-winning Pixar director behind *The Incredibles* films and *Ratatouille*, knows something about leading a big team to create something really amazing. But how do you get people to perform? Brad notes that if you have low morale, for every $1 you spend, you get about 25 cents of value. If you have high morale, for every $1 you spend, you get about $3 of value.

CEO Bob Iger shared his view about morale in the *Disney Newsreel*, the studio newsletter:

> ...I want Disney to be one of the most admired companies in the world, and we cannot do it without our employees. I want us to be admired by consumers, investors, and the general public, but I also want us to be admired by the people who know us best—our employees. **I want people to be proud to work here, to feel good about what we do and how we do it**...That's why it's so gratifying to hear that the vast majority of our employees are proud to work at Disney and that they feel respected here. Most have confidence in our strategic direction and our management, and more are engaged and empowered in their jobs. All of these things are critically important to our ability to achieve our goals as a company and to attract and retain the best talent.

In focusing on employee engagement and morale, let's look at some of the stories and factors that create deposits as well as withdrawals.

Labor Day Weekend 1971
LEADERS KNOW THE BEST WAYS TO ENGAGE OTHERS

When Disneyland opened up in 1955, it was the middle of July. In the days and weeks that followed, over a million people visited the park before the summer ended. It was a successful start to what would be known as *The Happiest Place on Earth*. But it was a crash course on managing huge numbers of Guests.

So when Walt Disney World opened with Magic Kingdom and its resorts, they decided to do it in the off season, allowing enough time to ramp up to prepare for the holidays and busier times of the year. October 1st, 1971 was chosen. But when you choose that date, you are preceded by another holiday—Labor Day. The park was under a tight schedule to open on time. It was all they could do to look ready by October 1st. Park and construction management decided that it was best to work through the holiday weekend. They went to the unions to explain. "We know that it's Labor Day and that it's a holiday weekend, but we need everyone working to get the park opened in time for October 1st!"

The response? "No."

"You don't understand. We are expecting crowds showing up on opening day. Press is coming from around the world. This thing will be televised. Everyone will be wondering if we have our act together. We have to work through Labor Day!"

The response? "You don't get it. It's Labor Day. We're not working!"

So Disney took a step back and reconsidered their approach. "If we can't get them to *work* on Labor Day, what if we had them *play* on Labor Day?"

So, they invited everyone involved in the construction of the Magic Kingdom to bring their family and be their Guest that Labor Day weekend. Management worked the park, utilizing new hires and opening every attraction that was ready for the Guests at that point.

Can you imagine the pride on the faces of those construction workers when that little daughter said, "Did you build that castle? It's beautiful! It's amazing!"

Can you also imagine the experience when one of those little kids said, "Hey, look at those subs from 20,000 Leagues Under the Sea! How cool is…wait a minute, they're not ready to ride yet? How come you haven't finished building that, Dad?!"

At the end of the experience, management told everyone involved with the construction of the park, "Get us open by October 1st, and when the construction is completed, we will get all of you back in to see the parks again for free."

Do you think the Magic Kingdom opened on time?

That story illustrates the difference between hard wiring and soft wiring. Most organizations want to be better than they are. Some do so successfully. World-class organizations—whether they are in the public, private, or non-profit sectors—have learned that there is a definitive link between highly satisfied customers and a highly engaged workforce. As a result, they look for ways to create a culture where employees are leaning forward in attaining the best possible results.

Hard Wiring Vs. Soft Wiring
LEADERS SOFT WIRE MORE THAN HARD WIRE

Often, in an attempt to raise the bar of excellence, organizations take certain actions. Some of those choices involve such moves as:

- Reconfiguring the organizational structure
- Reassigning or changing out managers
- Identifying new policies and procedures
- Creating new systems of accountability from databases to

performance plans

- Removing unproductive employees

Most of these efforts are referred to as Hard Wiring, in which we are establishing any number of activities and initiatives to generate employee compliance. Hard wiring as a technical term means a fixed, permanent connection between electrical and electronic components through wiring.

"Be wary of making too many rules." That's been the experience of Ed Catmull, President of Pixar Animation and Disney Animation. He states: "Rules can simplify life for managers, but they can be demeaning to the 95 percent who behave well. Don't create rules for the other 5 percent—address abuses of common sense individually."

There is perhaps a time and place for Hard Wiring. Often leaders institute such Hard Wiring efforts as establishing new policies and procedures, only to be dissatisfied that few substantive improvements come about as a result.

A better approach is to focus on Soft Wiring opportunities within the organization. What is Soft Wiring? Simply put, this is when we intentionally create a customer-centric culture that generates commitment. The advantages and benefits to Soft Wiring can often be far greater, as it:

- Often costs little or nothing to implement
- Takes less time to put into motion
- Furthers employee engagement
- Reduces our dependency on bureaucratic Hard Wiring measures that are in place
- Yields greater results over the long term
- Builds and deepens trust

Keep in mind that this is not some touchy feely activity. Gallup and other organizations have determined that it requires leadership excellence to engage employees to then drive organizational excellence. Soft Wiring will allow us to fuse those outcomes together and create the mission results we are seeking. Soft Wiring is a very intentional effort to move the culture of an organization to where it needs to be as it moves forward in a complex, competitive world. **Hard Wiring alone will not drive sustained results. But engineered thoughtfully, the addition of Soft Wiring can achieve a greater level of excellence than ever before.**

Let's look at how this plays out in the following examples.

Trashing the Poly
LEADERS ENCOURAGE RATHER THAN CONFRONT

A great example of what is meant by Hard Wiring comes from a story I heard about a general manager at Disney's Polynesian Resort. One day, he invited one of his front-line managers into his office. The manager stepped in, only to find trash all over the desk. Pointing to the garbage, the general manager inquired, "Do you know what this is?"

The front-line manager was baffled. "It looks like a lot of trash."

The general manager continued on to say something like this:

> This is what you walked by in the parking lot this morning when you went into the resort from your car. You stepped right by it and made no attempt to pick it up! I happened to come right behind you heading into work this morning, and saw you walk right by it. Now what I expect you to do is to get out there and clean up the rest of the parking lot!

This would be an example of Hard Wiring. In this instance, the general manager has given performance feedback to one of his managers about what is expected, and what should never happen. He has dramatically implied that what was done was inexcusable, and that it should never take place again.

But consider for a moment that perhaps there could have been a better approach. What if the general manager, upon noticing the individual walking past the trash, had called out to her in conversation? If the general manager then began picking up the trash as they spoke, it is pretty likely that the manager would have joined him. The conversation might have ended with, "Thanks for your help here. Hopefully our efforts in the parking lot will send a message to the team, to follow our lead."

Would the parking lot still get cleaned up?

Would the message about picking up trash you walked by get across?

Would you be modeling a better message of how to work in a more collegial manner, rather than being confrontational?

What's the message here? Real leadership consists of modeling more than confronting. That's Soft Wiring. Here's an example of Soft Wiring through modeling:

Thumbs Up on the Jungle Cruise
LEADERS MODEL EXPECTATIONS

Compare that experience to a long-told story I share in my book, *The Wonderful World of Customer Service at Disney*. One day, a Jungle Cruise pilot failed to notice that Walt Disney himself had joined the fellow passengers. In the early days of Disneyland, Walt would frequently walk around the park, observing the Guest experience by simply walking around. When the cruise was over, Walt stepped off the boat, and walked up to the one of the park's superintendents, Dick Nunis. "Dick, what's the trip time on this ride?" Nunis replied that it was seven minutes. "I just got a four-and-a-half-minute trip. How would you like to go to a movie and have the theater remove a reel in the middle of the picture?" Walt Disney continued, "Do you realize how much those hippos cost? I want people to see them, not be rushed through a ride by some guy who's bored with his work."

"Could I go on a trip with you?" Dick Nunis asked. Walt agreed to it. So Dick and Walt rode one of the boats through Adventureland and Walt demonstrated how to navigate the experience—"Speed up in the dull stretches, then slow down when you have something to look at." **Walt modeled what he expected of others.** He showed what the perfect voyage would look like. For a full week thereafter, the Jungle Cruise pilots were timed with stopwatches until they perfected the length of the ride. When Walt arrived for his regular visit to Disneyland on a subsequent weekend, he walked through Adventureland without stopping for a ride. He did the same the following weekend. After three weeks, he took a ride on one of the boats. When he returned to the dock, he entered the next boat for another ride. He went around four times, eliminating the possibility that the operators had "stacked the deck" by giving him the best pilots. When he emerged from the fourth trip, he turned to Dick Nunis and gave him a thumbs-up sign.

Since then, that thumbs-up sign has come to represent "great show" in providing Guest service in all of the Disney parks. **Recognition—even as simple as giving a thumbs up—is part of Soft Wiring**. So is training others. So is modeling the correct behavior. So is walking the park.

That brings us to another great way leaders can Soft Wire—not just by modelling but by mentoring.

Leaders of the Caribbean
LEADERS MENTOR OTHERS

Former Imagineer Tony Baxter was interviewed on an episode of the *Season Pass Podcast.* Tony had an amazing career that began by working at Disneyland, and then turned into a several decade career with Disney Imagineering. From Star Tours to Splash Mountain, from The Indiana Jones Adventure to heading up the team who designed Disneyland Paris, Tony had a career that would be envied by any Imagineering wannabe. What was fascinating to me was how he was mentored by Claude Coats. Claude Coats also had an amazing career; the highlight perhaps was designing the space that would become Pirates of the Caribbean.

After Walt's death, the work of designing and developing attractions for Disneyland and into the opening of Walt Disney World remained with the original generation of Imagineers. That group had been mentored by Walt Disney himself. **Mentoring others can be one of the greatest gifts of legacy you can give.** The problem is that this group was retiring and there wasn't any effort being made to bring in the next generation. The gift of being mentored has to be handed down from one generation to another.

Due to persistence and luck, Tony had the unique opportunity to become not only part of that next generation, but to be tutored under Claude Coats. Because of that opportunity, Tony learned many Imagineering concepts that helped him as an Imagineer in the years to come.

Tony also talks about the age gap between mentor and mentee. It worked for him, given that he was young and Claude was near retiring. He emphasizes the importance of there being an age gap between mentors and mentees so that there isn't a feeling of envy or jealousy by the mentor. Mentoring worked really well between Tony and Claude. And Tony has continued long after his career at Imagineering mentoring a new generation.

Who has mentored you? Who are you mentoring? Mentoring is so important in carrying the success of an organization from one generation to another. Tony will say that he owes much of his career to Claude. I would say that Claude's greatest legacy was not a specific ride or attraction, but the time he spent with Tony.

Leadership Voodoo in Department 510
LEADERS OWN THEIR RELATIONSHIPS WITH OTHERS

Soft Wiring also requires providing your employees the resources and support to be successful. An example of this was played out by a group in Imagineering known as Department 510.

Creating Epcot required an enormous army of individuals. Some of these individuals were artists and designers who, in their Imagineering roles, came up with the concepts and ideas for what Epcot would look like. The biggest team consisted of those who would construct the project. Engineers were those who bridged the gap between the designers and constructors. This was Department 510.

The biggest challenge of getting Epcot ready for opening day was not a technological problem, but a cultural one. The VP of Engineering, John Zovich, called this "the invisible stuff" or "the voodoo." To engineers, it might as well have been voodoo, and to one of their newest leaders, Art Frohwerk, it became obvious that the engineering division of WED (Imagineering's original name, based on the initials of Walter Elias Disney) wouldn't get anywhere until problems of getting along got sorted out.

Art Frohwerk soon found out after arriving at Disney that engineering was the most misunderstood and despised group in the entire Walt Disney organization. At the heart of the problem was an unhealthy dose of finger pointing within the organization. The creative group at WED would point at an engineer and complain that they hadn't listened to what was at the heart of the design or story, while the engineer would whine about the impracticality of the design—"I'm waiting on them for specs!" On the other end, the purchasing department was begging to get orders for materials like circuit boards, which had a painfully long lead time and were difficult to obtain. In exchange, Engineering was complaining about the fact that they hadn't gotten all the details yet.

Art knew that something needed to happen, and that it needed to begin with Engineering. He gathered the entire team together in two sessions to lay out a strategy. First, no more finger pointing. The success of this project was too critical for this team to hold onto petty grudges. **You can't improve relationships unless you take ownership for doing so.**

Having drawn a line in the sand, Art then provided a carrot at the end of the stick. The carrot was that Engineering would pay its employees to have lunch with others on the Mouse's dime. The stick was that those who went with them to lunch had to be "them"—their peers from other divisions within the company—storytellers, show designers, manufacturing, purchasing, planning, and so on.

Art set aside about $5,000 to make this happen, and initially, it worked. People were turning receipts in for having lunch with others. After a month or two, Art stopped getting expense reports; he wasn't sure what was happening—was he suddenly going to get hit up with a bunch of receipts? Finally, he asked the leadership team why he wasn't seeing any more receipts. No one said anything at first. Finally, one Imagineer, Linda, spoke up in the back of the room and said: "Art, we wouldn't charge the company to take our friends out to lunch." Building relationships had gone from the organized formality of meeting over lunch with members of other departments to the casual informality of simply hanging out and collaborating with others.

Art succeeded in breaking down the silos and in establishing working relationships throughout the organization. Some six months later, Department 510 was invited to a prestigious club high above Glendale. There, Ron Miller and other Disney executives celebrated the progress and turn-around that engineering had made, not only in organizing themselves for building Epcot, but in their becoming better team players. Each received a shirt with a graphic that stated "I love 510" with Mickey peering over the top. The number 510 refers to the name of their department. Department 510 had learned to collaborate, explain itself, and facilitate whatever it took to pull off the mission.

Soon after this, Dept. 510 had its own visioning session to reflect on what it had achieved. It became known from within that they: "Pick up where dreams left off."

Working Out the Bugs
LEADERS PROVIDE A WORK/LIFE BALANCE

Attaining excellence isn't easy—even for Pixar. That was made clear to the folks at Pixar. Imagine having achieved the first full-length computer animated film, *Toy Story*. This was a huge triumph. But the celebration was short-lived because they now needed to go right into production on *A Bug's Life*. Making a film on bugs turned out to be harder than expected and involved a different level of detail. Plus, they were trying to get down the processes of working as a studio. So there was plenty of work to be done.

Meanwhile, with *Toy Story's* success, Disney wanted a sequel. The initial plan was to do it direct-to-video. But then John Lasseter realized that he didn't want to have two standards of quality at the studio, so he decreed that the story be retooled into a full-length feature.

The problem is that when Pixar told Disney that it planned to start over, Disney objected, saying that the distribution process—which usually took a couple of years—was already set in motion. McDonalds was even planning on doing Happy Meal toys. In Disney's view, there was no changing the date. And that date was only nine months away—a nearly impossible deadline.

That's when chaos really set in. Employees who had spent years in overdrive had to work even harder. In the Pixar history, *To Infinity and Beyond*, the general consensus at the studio is that *Toy Story 2's* production was fueled by a nine-month long adrenaline rush, induced alternately by both panic and excitement.

That kind of work brought some serious consequences, according to Sarah McArthur, Pixar's head of production:

We learned that people at Pixar would literally give everything they had for a film. If we asked them, they would give and not hold anything back. And because they didn't hold back, people were hurt.

Some staff hit the wall. A full third of the staff experienced the effects of carpal tunnel syndrome from doing repeated physical routines. The ultimate moment was when an exhausted animator set off to work with the intent of dropping off his infant child at daycare. Later in the day, while on the phone with his wife, he realized that he had never dropped the child off and that the baby had been left forgotten in the back seat. Rushing out to the car, they found the baby unconscious and poured cold water over him immediately. Fortunately, the baby was okay. But the experience was a wake-up call.

The deadlines were met, and the films were enormously successful. The films that followed afterward also had tight deadlines. But it did mean that the company had to stop and think about what really mattered. It instituted a medical team, along with massage therapists. Ergonomic furniture was brought in, and a gym was opened with yoga and tai chi classes. In addition, the company resolved not only to curb overtime, but to make sure deadlines were realistic. Many of the outcomes of this near catastrophic experience have led to shaping Pixar's culture today—one that believes that its people are truly its greatest assets.

Leadership & You

As a leader, consider the following:

- Am I always resorting to organizational restructuring in order to create some needed change?

- Am I always adding policies and procedures to make sure things happen the way I want them to?

- Are my employees tiring from change that really doesn't

result in real improvement?

- How can I work alongside others to model & inspire the behavior I desire of them?

- Are there opportunities for me to mentor others?

- Who is mentoring me?

- How do I keep people from pointing fingers at others?

- What resources can I provide to help others get along?

- How do I provide for balance in the lives of my employees?

- What systems and resources have I put in place to create for balance in the workplace?

10

I Am Like a Little Bee
Leaders Build Trust & Empower Others

Walt Disney was stumped one day when a little boy asked, "Do you draw Mickey Mouse?"

> I had to admit I do not draw anymore. "Then you think up all the jokes and ideas?" "No," I said, "I don't do that." Finally he looked at me and said, "Mr. Disney, just what do you do?" "Well," I said, "sometimes I think of myself as a little bee. I go from one area of the studio to another and gather pollen and sort of stimulate everybody. I guess that's the job I do."

Walt's philosophy revolved around developing and nurturing others. His strength was not that he created those amazing animated classics himself frame by frame, but that he gathered a creative team and empowered them to do their very best. And not just in an individual contribution. The secret is to create a unified group effort. Each character is drawn and brought to life through many hands. It is what others have called the "Disney Touch."

Three Branches of Trust
Leaders Embrace a Culture of Trust

Empowering others to come together to create that "Disney Touch" requires first and foremost, trust. Consider how this plays out in one of Walt Disney's greatest film classics, *Swiss Family Robinson*, released in 1960. From the film comes three stories of trust:

The first one comes from the movie itself. One of the great messages in Disney's classic film, *Swiss Family Robinson*, centers on trust. This was portrayed in the difference between the father (John Mills) and the mother (Dorothy McGuire). Trusting to go to New Guinea in the first place; trusting to leave the ship after it was wrecked and not wait for immediate rescue; trusting in leaving the beach and seeking a home in the jungle; trusting their youngest boy Francis (Kevin Corcoran) to be up in the tree during construction; trusting their two oldest boys Fritz and Ernst (James MacArthur and Tommy Kirk) to set out on their own on a raft looking for others; and finally, trusting to remain on the island and build a life for themselves when help arrived and the option to return back was presented. Note that the word "courage" could have been used in every instance that we used the word "trust". **Being courageous enough to trust, and having the trust to be courageous goes hand in hand.**

The second story centers on Walt's production of the film. He authorized his biggest budget ever for a live-action feature at that time—a sum of $4,500,000—to create the film. But Walt trusted his director Ken Annakin, to go out to the island of Tobago and do a 22 week on-location shoot where water, animal actors, and weather all factored into making production longer and more expensive. "Such a great story as the Swiss Family Robinson deserves every penny we spent on it."

The six-month shoot was not without its challenges. A crew of nearly 1,000 worked to construct roads, storm shelters, cooking and dining facilities, parking lots, and even a makeshift soundstage. Some 500 animals were shipped in to include eight dogs, two giant tortoises, 40 monkeys, two elephants, six ostriches, four zebras, 100 flamingos, six hyenas, two anacondas, and a tiger.

Even the actors had to apply some trust to their situation. In true

British humor, John Mills described the difficulties:

> If a scorpion doesn't bite me during the night, I get into
> the car, and if it doesn't skid off the edge of a cliff, I reach
> the mangrove swamp. I walk through; and if I'm not
> sucked in by quicksand, eaten alive by land crabs, or bitten
> by a snake, I reach the beach. I change on the beach,
> trying to avoid being devoured by insects, and walk into
> the sea. If there are no sharks or barracudas about, we get
> the shot and then do the whole thing in reverse, providing
> of course, we haven't died of sunstroke in the meantime.

In the end, all of that and more didn't matter; because the result
was that the film was the highest grossing Disney film of 1960,
eventually bringing some $40,000,000 into the studio coffers.
With the added success of *The Absent-Minded Professor*, *101
Dalmatians*, and *The Parent Trap* during that same time, Walt and
Roy were able to, for the first time in the history of their
company, pay off the long-term loan they had held from Bank of
America. Now, revenue from the motion pictures would go
directly back to the studio instead of the bank.

Finally, the third story comes from the operation of the Swiss
Family Treehouse attraction at the Magic Kingdom.

I had a colleague at Disney who, in her college years, started out
in Adventureland attractions. One night she was working at the
entrance to the Swiss Family Treehouse, taking B-ticket coupons
from the Guests, though few were coming through by that hour of
the evening. At one point, several young men approached her and
started asking a couple of questions. That led to a short dialogue
with them about where they were from and of their trip to
Orlando. Out of the corner of her eye, she noticed a very
prominent Walt Disney World executive pass by. She didn't think
too much of it, and then a few moments later, the young men
went their way.

A little while later, this same senior official came by and chewed
her out left and right for talking to and flirting with the young

men. She was completely surprised by his demeanor. She in no way was flirting, nor did she bring on the interaction. She was simply politely answering their questions, all the while handling the greeter position she had been assigned to. She had never met the executive before, nor did he know anything of her, and yet he assumed she was "slacking off" and not doing her job. It was difficult in the years that followed to really have any sense of respect for this individual after his angry demonstration toward her that evening.

That same executive had received ample trust from Walt Disney when he was a young manager. And yet, years later he couldn't apply that same trust and empowerment to a front-line Cast Member doing her job.

None of us will ever experience surviving a shipwreck and having to establish your life on a lonely island. **Few, if any, of us will have the opportunity to produce or direct an expensive film production, much less live on a stranded island. Most of us, however, will be in a position where we will have to trust the co-workers around us. How we respond matters.**

Purchasing Trust at the Emporium
LEADERS CALCULATE THE COST OF MISTRUST

The Emporium on Main Street, U.S.A. is a big part of the park experience, whether you are in Anaheim, Orlando, Tokyo, Paris, or Hong Kong. Who of us hasn't stopped and made a purchase on the way out after a big day at the parks? When I was with the Walt Disney World Company, it was said that more business at the Emporium occurred in the last couple of hours at the park than the entire rest of the day combined. It was also said that the sales per square footage of those stores far exceeded what could be sold in the comparable square footage of any major department store.

My favorite Emporium is in Disneyland Paris. Not so much

because of the merchandise, but because of a unique antique found in the center of the store. Because theming is so replete in this park, one may pass by barely noticing its existence. But if you have the opportunity, head inside and take a closer look, because it says so much about trust.

In the center of the store is a device actually used in stores like this a century ago. The purpose of this device is to make change for each purchase. According to Eddie Soto, former Imagineer and show producer responsible for Main Street, U.S.A. at Disneyland Paris, they found this invention through research photos. In the old days, cashiers were not trusted to handle change. They would take the money, place it in a basket with the sales slip, pull the rope, and it went on a track upstairs, where management would make the change, and then send the basket back downstairs to the customer.

Imagine if that were the status quo at the Emporium today. Lines at the end of the day would go back to the castle with Guests waiting to make their purchase. If any store followed that sort of thinking, they would lose significant business. Fortunately, technology, if not trust, evolves.

There's an adage that says:

> *"A manager whose business went bust*
> *Shook his head and exclaimed in disgust:*
> *'Employees are inept.*
> *So I checked their every step.*
> *And I got killed by high costs of low trust.'"*

A wise man, whose work I respected, said, **"I would rather live my life largely trusting others—and then at times be disappointed—than to live my life largely as a cynic."**

You may not have to build a tree house in the jungle, or step inside an old-fashioned emporium to do business, but the next time you put processes, rules, or procedures in place to ensure trust, consider this question: What will this look like 25, 50, or 100 years from now?

The Tom Murphy School of Management
LEADERS GIVE PEOPLE THE SPACE TO SUCCEED

Separating Steering from Rowing can be found in what Iger referred to as The Tom Murphy School of Management. Tom Murphy was chairman and chief executive officer of Capital Cities/ABC until Disney purchased it in 1996. But up until that time, he was a great mentor to Bob Iger, who would later become CEO of Disney. Bob looks at his role this way:

"In a strange way, I am the brand manager of Disney." In an article with *Fortune*, he noted that his job is, in the words of his friend, the late Steve Jobs, more "brand deposits" than "brand withdrawals."

Warren Buffet says of Iger, "Bob is just very effective. He's always calm and rational and makes sense, and therefore he gets things done through other people. He runs things without a heavy hand."

Stated Jay Rasulo, CFO at the time:

> I've heard Bob say more than once, **"If I can't trust a person to do that, then I need a different person." And so we are empowered to basically run those business areas.** I would say that Bob has a states vs. federal philosophy.

Bob Iger himself calls it The Tom Murphy School of Management. "You put good people in jobs and give them room to run. You involve yourself in a responsible way, but not to the point where you are usurping their authority. I don't have the time or concentration—and you could argue maybe even the talent—to do that."

The Fairest Trust in the Land
LEADERS TRUST OTHERS TO DO THEIR WORK

Known in the early years as Snow White's Adventures, the "dark ride" attraction opened at the Magic Kingdom in 1971 along with Peter Pan's Flight and Mr. Toad's Wild Ride. Originally, *Sleeping Beauty*, *Mary Poppins*, and *The Legend of Sleepy Hollow* were intended to be the themes for these three attractions. But as costs increased while building the original Walt Disney World Resort, it was necessary to find some shortcuts. Re-using the same attraction themes from Disneyland seemed to make sense at the time.

Building the attraction was not so easy. **Like the queen peering down at Snow White from her castle tower, it's hard to whistle while you work when managers are staring down at you, looking at your every move.**

Such was the case for Arrow Development, a third-party contractor Disney hired to help create some of the first attraction vehicles built for the Magic Kingdom. Ships flying over Neverland, Skyway buckets, flying Dumbos, spinning teacups, and cars veering through "nowhere in particular" were just a small part of what Arrow created for the Magic Kingdom. Included in all this were the original mine carts slated for Snow White's Adventures.

But as work progressed on building all of these rides and attractions, corporate started sending people out of California to look over everything and make sure it was going smoothly. For Arrow, these people didn't facilitate their success. They simply stood in the way of getting the job done, by asking questions about schedules and budgets. **It's generally difficult for anyone to do their work with a big "Heigh-Ho" when management is looking over your shoulder all the time.**

And it wasn't like Arrow was some new kid on the block. Arrow had worked personally with Walt Disney to create many of the rides and attractions that opened at Disneyland back in 1955. Arrow had even pioneered the first bobsleds to roll down the first steel roller coaster that had ever been built. They had long proved themselves over the years.

Fortunately, there was one person Arrow could turn to for the help they needed. Once again, that man was Joe Fowler, whose "can do" attitude was discussed earlier in this book. Joe and Arrow had worked together for many years. And now Joe was on site and over much of the massive construction project.

Joe trusted Arrow to get the job done. So when people from Burbank and Anaheim came over and started giving Arrow Development trouble, they would just call Joe and say, "Can you get these guys off our back?" and five minutes later, they were gone. Fowler would send those middlemen to some other end of the park or property, because he knew that his best chance for getting all of the attractions opened by October 1, 1971 was to trust Arrow with the freedom and space they needed to get the job accomplished.

Steering vs. Rowing
LEADERS ALLOW OTHERS TO STEER OR ROW

This business of looking over people's shoulders and telling them every little thing they should do is what I refer to as Steering vs. Rowing. As a new Disney Cast Member, I remember anticipating my participation in Canoe Races of the World (C.R.O.W.). It was a Cast Member activity & tradition that dates back several decades. Dozens of teams would sign up, usually from different parts of the operation. There would be some group representing Disney's Caribbean Beach Resort, one group of French Cast Members from World Showcase, while another group represented skippers from the Jungle Cruise.

I was with The Disney Institute and was excited to organize a team. I tried to drum up a team, but unfortunately, most of my colleagues had been around Disney for years. For them, it was "been there, done that." Instead, I managed to sign up with a group from the island of misfit Cast Members throughout the property wanting to be part of a team. The only thing we shared in common was our excitement for participating in the canoe races.

These events were done over several days, and all before the Guests entered the park. I remembered entering the backstage area behind Frontierland while it was barely light. The races started organizing just after 6 a.m. A little fog was coming off the Rivers of America, and it seemed that you were truly in a magical frontier. No Guests, just the quiet of the morning, and Cast Members gathering from all over.

There were no practice runs, which gave our team little opportunity to get to know each other or even figure out how to work together as a team. In that moment it didn't matter. After all, it was really about having fun.

When it came our turn, we eagerly boarded our canoes, and rowed out to the starting line, which is approximately the space between the current rafts to Tom Sawyer Island, and the island dock itself. You would row against another team, but your success in moving up was based on your overall time. We were on the outside lane. Not ideal, but we were enthused and ready to win.

The whistle was blown and off we paddled! We rowed hard. We knew that success was dependent on everyone rowing in unison, so we were all very focused on timing our paddles together so that we would maximize speed. And speed we did. We were paddling so hard that we quickly out-stroked the other team by nearly a canoe's length within only a few seconds after starting.

And then, wham! We hit rock! Actually, what we hit was a cement shore painted like rock. We looked up, only to realize that we indeed had hit Big Thunder Mountain and ran up the shore! It was then that we realized we were all so focused on moving as fast as we could, that none of us were paying attention to where we were going! It was all rowing and no steering!

We beached so hard on the shore that we couldn't paddle backward. In fact, a few had to get out of the front of the canoe to lighten the weight and push the canoe back into the water. We went on to finish the race, but make no mistake about it. Our efforts won the record for the worst time ever in canoe paddling history!

We all kept a great sense of humor about it in the end, and my canoeing experience taught me a powerful lesson: **You must separate the duties of steering from rowing.** For those of you who remember the canoes at the Magic Kingdom, or who still get to enjoy them at Disneyland, you'll recall that there are two Cast Members for every canoe. One of those Cast Members takes the lead in getting everyone to row and to do so in sync. But the other sits in the rear. Their job is not to row the canoe, but to steer the canoe in the direction it should go.

The same is true of any good organization. We need people who can steer, and we need people who can row. Steering requires people who can see the big picture. These are individuals who can look across the landscape of issues and possibilities and can identify opportunities and strategies for moving forward. Rowing, on the other hand, requires those people who are good at focusing intently on one mission and in performing that mission well. Those leaders who row are working to make their efforts succeed by coming together as a team. Those leaders who steer are always looking to find the best ways to achieve their goals. Both are needed.

Too often, we put very capable people on jobs and expect them to row, when they really could be putting their attention best to steering the organization in the direction it should go. Unfortunately, we don't get to see them doing their best, because they are strapped down in the minutia of jobs and tasks that have little bearing on where the organization should be going. Steering is very difficult when the organization's best strategists are devoted to rowing.

Institutionally, there is a time and place for steering and rowing. But world-class organizations separate the work of rowing from steering. Too often, management and executives want to "pick up the paddles" and make things happen themselves—or at least dictate what they should be. Rather, the emphasis should be on putting that strategy and foundation in place, then supporting their teams in helping them be their very best in rowing toward the finish line.

At Nordstrom and other world-class organizations, this is presented as turning the organizational pyramid upside down. This is not some act of organizational restructuring as such, but rather, a philosophy that asks, how can we support our direct reports in providing the best customer experience possible? Consider those leadership behaviors that would be most conducive to supporting and engaging employees. Gallup and others have consistently found that if management can support employees in the work they have to do, the domino effect will be to create greater employee performance.

Leadership & You

As a leader, consider the following:

- Who do I trust? Do I trust others? Do I trust myself? Do others trust me?

- What are the hidden costs behind mistrust?

- What are the inherent rewards in showing trust?

- How am I avoiding the impression of looking over someone's shoulder?

- How am I at building trusting, collaborative relationships with others?

- How will giving people greater space and freedom to do their job provide assurance that the job will get done?

- How do I balance freedom and accountability?

11

EVERYONE PICKS UP TRASH
LEADERS FLATTEN THE ORGANIZATION

We previously spoke of Hard and Soft Wiring. Flattening the organization can hold the promise of creating a more dynamically functioning team. But the approach I speak of here is not so much about some organizational change, as much as it is about a paradigm shift, where the culture of the organization is so flat, that "everyone picks up trash."

Where "Kings are Commoners and Commoners are Kings"
LEADERS DO MORE THAN PROVIDING AN OPEN DOOR POLICY

Written decades ago, a quotation in *Walt Disney's Disneyland* has a message still relevant today. The section was titled: "Kings are Commoners and Commoners are Kings."

It alludes largely to the royalty who have visited Disneyland. By this point in the park's history, a wide variety of VIPs had visited the park. Here's a quote from that particular section:

> But the fundamental reason for the king-commoner analogy is found in the basic approach to entertaining its Guests that is practiced at Disneyland. Here, hosts and hostesses strive to live up to a credo contained in the training manual at the University of Disneyland, a real classroom school that all who work here attend: "We love

to entertain kings and queens, but the vital thing to remember is this—*every* Guest receives the VIP treatment."

That same kind of thinking works well if you think about your own group of employees. Many managers talk about an "open door" policy. **Consider the possibility that as a leader, if you require a door, you *don't* have an "open door" policy.** A better experience is to have management out in the cubicles with their team. Use the rooms with doors for meetings that might need to be held from time to time in private. But make the regular day-to-day activity happen out in the trenches.

That's the spirit behind creating a "flattened" organization. That's not to say that Walt wasn't clearly on top and in charge. Recall earlier when he wondered aloud if he wasn't the last of the benevolent dictators. In a previous management era where the management philosophy was "my way or the highway", there was really no roadmap for creating a flatter organization. But he certainly wasn't interested in being held to some royal treatment. His focus wasn't on structure—it was in achieving unbelievable results.

Problems at the Penthouse
LEADERS CREATES OPPORTUNITIES FOR ALL

In the early days at the Hyperion Studios, there was a real sense of collegiality. Artist Ken Peterson started as an assistant animator on *Snow White and the Seven Dwarfs*. He described the feeling at the time as follows:

> I was at Hyperion for four years, and we were all one happy family. It was a wonderful time, people coming from all over, all funny guys, offbeat. We'd lunch "on the [drawing] board" and go out and play touch football in Griffith Park on the noon hour. There wasn't anybody you couldn't ask for help, a top animator or whoever. There were different salaries, but nobody worried about that. We all figured we were learning something and it was true.

With the success of *Snow White*, Walt Disney decided to take the profits and reinvest it in building an ideal studio that would be just right for his staff. The layout of the building branched outward, optimizing the opportunity to be as close to natural light as possible, with as many rooms facing north as possible. Venetian blinds could be adjusted to lessen the glare.

Animation desks for the artists were designed not only for efficiency, but also for the comfort of the animators themselves. Carpets and pastel colors would provide a soothing atmosphere.

Outside there were broad lawns where employees could play baseball, badminton, or volleyball during lunch hours. The studio cafeteria served meals below the studio's cost, with deliveries made to any worker too busy to get it for themselves.

Then, there was the Penthouse. A sort of gentlemen's club that included a lounge, soda fountain, sun deck, gymnasium, and showers. No alcohol. And you'd get a second glance if Walt found out you were spending too much time up there. But that wasn't the biggest problem with the Penthouse. As Ken Peterson described:

> When we moved to the new studio, Walt's paternalism was expressed in the Penthouse Club. The dividing line for membership was money; you had to earn two hundred a week, something like that. I didn't qualify and a lot of others didn't either.

> When the union came in, I don't think any of us knew anything about unions. But we were all feeling sort of left out...the strike was about economics, but it was also a rebellion about the kind of management Walt had.

That sense of "royal" treatment would bring Walt to experience one of the most painful episodes of his career. When a strike was fully launched, Walt took it personally, and perhaps understandably so. After all, so much of the profits were applied toward creating a better space for everyone to enjoy. He probably didn't see the effect that one little "club" could have on the entire culture. Even he himself, while having an office suite, had a working arrangement that was very modest compared to the Hollywood moguls of that time.

Walt was angry with those who participated in the strike. Moreover, he was personally hurt. Hadn't he used his resources to improve the employee experience? Couldn't they see that he cared? **The truth is, in providing favorite employees exclusive perks, you soon create segmentation. And with segmentation comes resentment.**

At the height of the strike, Walt was sent off by the United States government on a goodwill tour of South America while his brother Roy settled matters. While he was gone, their father Elias passed away. A few months later, the U.S. went into World War II and many of the artists left to go serve. For Walt, it would never be quite the same afterward.

There is Only One Mr. Toad
LEADERS ARE NOT CONCERNED WITH TITLES

Still, Walt persisted in creating the right environment for his employees—especially as he built Disneyland. One of the traditions he put in place was that everyone—including himself— was to go on a first name basis. Renie Bardeau, Disneyland's photographer, shared:

> One morning I was sitting in the interior dining room of Hills Bros. Coffee Shop, when Walt walked in and looked around for a place to sit. I was the only one in there and he walked up and asked, "Mind if I sit down?"

> "No, of course not, sit right down, Walt." He asked me a couple of questions about the Park. We had met before and it surprised me that he remembered my name.

> Suddenly a waitress showed up and asked, "Can I help you, Mr. Disney?"

Walt replied, "Yes, but remember, I'm Walt. There's only one 'mister' in Disneyland and that's Mr. Toad."

Only the Mouseketeers referred to him as Uncle Walt. To everyone else, it was Walt, not Mr. Disney. It was more than an informal title. It was really a way that Walt Disney approached his work. Late in Walt's life, Dean Jones recalled one incident that underscores this philosophy that every individual was equal in Walt's mind:

> A gardener at the Disney studio left some tools in an empty parking space. When a producer drove up and saw the tools in his space, he honked at the gardener and gave the poor man a chewing-out. Walt walked up and interrupted the producer's tirade. "Hold it!" he said. "Don't you ever treat one of my employees like this. This man's been with me longer than you have, so you'd better be good to him!"

The Orange Tie Debacle
LEADERS PITCH IN

Walt once complained that he couldn't find a supervisor when he wanted one while at Disneyland. He even resisted providing management fancy offices backstage in fear that they would spend their entire time there and not out in the park.

So, in a move that would again create a hierarchy, one of the park heads came up with the idea for all supervisors to wear orange ties so as to be easily recognized. This was not well received by most of the other employees. The thought was you can have a hundred good supervisors, but all you need is one miserable manager and then all of the others are labeled with the symbol of an orange tie. Soon, orange ties had come to represent a miserable "Peeping Tom" type of supervision.

Fortunately, the ties eventually went away. **Subtle symbols at work can often separate management from the main**

body of employees. The symbol of an orange tie had separated those in charge from the rest of the Cast. Yet, with a tie or not, the notion persists in any organization, even Disney's.

Since then, one way that Disney management supports the Cast is by taking on front line roles during peak season periods. Even the company's Christmas parties in the past have had senior executives like Michael Eisner serving hot dogs on Main Street, U.S.A. The idea is to get people out of the office and into the front line where they can appreciate the work that goes on there, while improving the delivery to the customer during peak times.

That's not to say there haven't been further efforts to make the organization more vertical over the years. When the Team Disney building was created in Burbank under Eisner, it had a separate executive dining room. Those kinds of arrangements and furnishings often send the wrong message.

Autopian Approval
LEADERS GO OUT OF THEIR WAY FOR OTHERS

It doesn't take a big organizational restructuring to send a message about flattening the organization. What it does take is leadership. Take, for example, the experience of Bob Gurr creating the first car for the Autopia attraction. He had created a full-size clay model, called a "clay buck." Based on approval of that design, they would then create the mold for the actual car body.

The clay buck was built in the garage of a teacher from Pasadena's Art Center College of Design. Students volunteered time to help design it. Once built, it was so big and heavy that it was going to be very hard to move without cracking it. Bob needed Walt's approval, but how could he get this thing to the studio? New to the company, he figured a big important studio head would never come over to someone's garage.

So, Bob asked Walt if he could bring the clay model over to the studio for approval. Walt said, "You're going to bring that big heavy thing over here, just so I can look at it? Nonsense. We can all drive there in a few minutes." They piled into a car and headed over to the garage. Once there, Walt walked around the clay buck, checking it from every angle. Then he sat down in it. The clay was still sticky, so Walt ended up with clay all over his jacket. He was a mess, but he approved the car for production.

In the words of Bob Gurr:

> **I never saw Walt act like a big shot. He had high standards of excellence, but he was never demanding. He never wanted people to go out of their way just to serve him. Fact is, he would go out of his way to save time for us, and that made everything go more smoothly.**

Via Jeff Kurtti's book on Disney Imagineering Legends, Bob Gurr recalls another incident with Walt and Joe Fowler:

> The three of us walked into the drugstore at the Sheraton Hotel in Pittsburgh to get a cheeseburger. In the store, Walt noticed that the merchandise rack had the Disney merchandise down on the bottom. So he said something like, "Come on, boys. Let's fix this!" If you can, imagine the three of us fully grown men, down on our knees, picking up the Disney merchandise and the sales tags off the bottom racks, and putting them up on the top, and then putting whatever merchandise was up there back down on the lower one. And a sales lady comes over and, very obstinately, says, "May I help you?" Walt says, "No, we're all done here." And then we went over to get our cheeseburgers.

Years later, Bob was invited by other studio staff to visit. As he headed toward the salad bar to grab something to eat, he was pleasantly surprised to see Bob Iger making a salad for himself. That kind of behavior—where a CEO can be found among the employees getting lunch for himself like anyone else—hearkens back to Walt's own preference of grabbing a bowl of chili and sitting among the employees, rather than hobnobbing among the VIPs and press. **Little things can create that sense of a flattened organization.**

And big things—particularly managers at the top--can prevent it.

Powers That Be on a Monorail
LEADERS IMPART KNOWLEDGE AND UNDERSTANDING

One of the things that happens when the culture is not flat is that the front line loses understanding around why decisions are what they are. Here's an example of this. For some time, the monorail express line from the Magic Kingdom back to TTC (Transportation & Ticket Center) had been closed off during the morning hours. The express monorail was working, but they wouldn't board anyone who wanted to head back to the TTC.

I asked a front line Cast Member why the monorails weren't working. He said they had gone 101, meaning one or more were failing to operate. I then asked why there was a policy that the express return was never available in the morning hours from the Magic Kingdom? He turned to another Cast Member who then turned to another front line worker. None of them knew. They then called their supervisor. Struggling to connect via radio with that manager, I learned that the individual was at the TTC, and I stated that I would seek out the manager when I got there.

I found the manager at the TTC. The individual couldn't have been more professional. But he didn't have a reason as to why they didn't open up the express return from the Magic Kingdom in the mornings. He conjectured that it might be a security issue, because he had tried to open it on one occasion and security had locked that exit on the far right leading to the monorail platform (security was being handled at the entrance to the Magic Kingdom at the time). I asked if this was about two silos not working together—security and transportation? He said he wasn't sure, and he called a Guest service manager to come.

The Guest service manager was also very professional. Both of these gentlemen seemed like two people who were good people to work with and for. I articulated all of my frustrations about the monorail system, but was very clear about my ongoing frustration that the Magic Kingdom entrance was closed most mornings to the express monorail. After listening to me, his response could best be summed up as follows:

"I'm sorry, that's a decision that's made by the 'powers that be'."

He said that those "powers that be" make any number of decisions about testing, about opening and closing and so forth, and that this was one of those decisions. These managers weren't included in the decisions, nor did he know specifically why they had decided that. He couldn't state what the reasoning or rationale was, or how they got to that decision. It was simply a decision made by the powers that be.

I have learned for myself that there are red flags when an employee states, "I don't know. It was decided by the powers that be!" Three levels of the organization, and no one had an official reason for why. I'm not even sure any of them felt comfortable going up the ladder and asking "Why?"

The response couldn't have been more disconcerting. When you say "upper management made that decision" or "it came from the top" or it was decided by the "powers that be", it usually suggests any and/or all the following:

- The powers that be may be clueless as to what is really happening on the front line.

- The powers that be have not involved the front line in the decision making process.

- The powers that be have not done a good job communicating the "why" in their decision.

- The powers that be probably do not have a good "why" that they would want to have explained to their Guests.

- The powers that be probably do not see the impact of the

decision on the Guest experience.

- The powers that be probably have not made a good decision, and therefore, don't want to have to defend it. "Because we said so" becomes the replacement.

And here's what becomes a casualty in this. You will have employees–Cast Members, in this case– who do not feel informed and engaged. The trickle-down effect is that you will have Guests feeling unsatisfied by the experience and not really understood.

Now, lest you think this is just about jumping all over Walt Disney World transportation, this same "powers that be" problem exists in all manner of organizations, from hospitals to banks to government agencies. But when you hear that the policy can't be explained because of upper management, it's for all of the reasons bulleted earlier. So this is about any organization as well as Disney's. It's important to make sure that you don't just go with the status quo because that was what the "powers that be" decided. **When people say "the powers that be", you have essentially failed to flatten and engage your organization.**

Everyone Picks Up Trash
LEADERS GET IN THE TRENCHES

The previous example is not what makes Disney successful. Rather, Disney is rooted in traditions that are much more flattened. For instance, one of the first things new Cast Members are taught on Day 1 of their orientation, Disney Traditions, is that "everyone picks up trash." I learned this firsthand when I attended my orientation. My Traditions leader, Claudio Diaz, took us on a tour of the Magic Kingdom. The park was pretty clean, but when we got to the Partners statue of Walt Disney and Mickey Mouse, I remember him picking up cigarette butts lined up in the container garden with his bare fingers. That made an unmistakable impression on me.

This tradition stems from Walt Disney himself. There are even images of him picking up trash in the park during the early days of Disneyland. And it has continued to this day. Tim Delaney, responsible for the development of Tomorrowland at Disneyland Paris, shared his experience with the *Season Pass Podcast*:

> So we're walking along. We start to walk out of Discoveryland. Frank [Wells, then President of the Walt Disney Company], my wife and I are walking along. Frank was so proud of the park. And he stops and he reaches down and picks up a piece of trash and throws it away. So he says like, "Yeah, I'm so excited about the park, you guys have done a great job," and he stops again. And he picks up a cigarette butt and throws it away. He's like: "What is the matter with these people? How can they mess up our park?"
>
> So he says, "Hold on a second." So he walks over to one of the drink carts and he gets two cups. And he goes "Come on, Tim. We're going to clean up the park." So, here he is in his dark blue suit. This tall elegant guy. So we walk, and my wife peels off to the side, and we walk out of Discoveryland, into the center hub, down Main Street, U.S.A., all the way down Main Street toward the train station. And he and I are picking up trash. And he's like, "What's the matter with these people?" How can they throw trash on the ground in our park?' He was just impassioned about this.
>
> So we get to the end of Main Street, U.S.A., and there's a merchant cart. **There's a Cast Member standing next to the merchandise cart, and Frank's walking around picking up trash and putting it in this cup. And I said to her: "Don't mind him, he's just the president of the Walt Disney Company."** And so we throw this stuff away, and we go into the bathroom and we're washing our hands, and then we come on out and he goes, "Well, I got to go. I got a meeting to go to." And Frank starts running off. I mean literally--he goes jogging off. That's what he did...And he

goes bounding off to this meeting. And I stood there. And I watched him disappear. He ran through the train station and left. And I said to myself, "We will never fail." ...That kind of commitment was so extraordinary. I was really touched by that. It meant a lot. It really meant a lot. That commitment was not just lip service commitment, but physical commitment, and passion for what he was doing.

Everyone Picks Up Trash. It's not just about keeping a park clean. It's about flattening an organization.

Leadership & You

As a leader, consider the following:

- How do people refer to each other in the organization? Are titles formal or informal?

- Does my treatment of others—regardless of rank—suggest that title does not matter?

- What employee benefits or special treatment ends up separating people, rather than bring them together?

- What does a "peeping Tom" approach of management look like in my organization?

- Do we as managers set ourselves apart from others or do we get in the trenches and work with those around us?

- What systems are in place to call on support from others during peak times and to get "all hands on deck"?

- Is the decision making based on "the powers that be"?

- What behaviors like "everyone picks up trash" suggest that the organization is a flattened one?

12

GET ON THE BUS
LEADERS GET EVERYBODY ON BOARD

My Mickey School Bus Lunchbox
LEADERS GET ON THE BUS

I spent a childhood studying Walt Disney, the man. I dreamed about being an animator, producer, and Imagineer. I loved the stories of creativity and imagination, and fancied myself saving Walt Disney Productions at the time, an organization needing a hero in the seventies and early eighties.

When I was originally hired in the 1990s, I was immediately tasked with producing a large video series for The Disney Institute. The timing was tight, as the Institute would lose its budget if the work was not completed by the end of the fiscal year. In completing that assignment, I was gone days, if not weeks, at a time from the office, focused on filming throughout the parks. I had little time to get to know others and to build relationships with my new peers.

Even upon completion of that project, I was responsible for completing other key projects. I worked hard and was successful in the work I accomplished. At the same time, I had little to do with a new supervisor who had stepped in and knew very little of what I was working on. Conversely, I knew little of what she was focused on. In retrospect, we were probably not very aligned.

After a couple years at Disney, I was invited to attend a weeklong leadership program designed for newly hired Disney leaders during their first year. Unfortunately, my schedule had been so tight I had been incapable of finding time to attend. When I finally signed up, I, along with the other participants from across the company, were given 360 evaluations of our performance. If you are not familiar with a 360, it's essentially a survey you take, along with your peers, the customers (clients) you serve, and your supervisor. All of this is intended to give you a sense of how people see you in terms of your results and your ability to effectively work with others.

On the first afternoon of the program, we were shown a video of Judson Green, president of Walt Disney Attractions, who talked about "getting on the bus." What that meant was that the company was trying to be more collaborative, and not operate from a "my way or the highway" mentality. At the end of the day, we were given the results of the 360 surveys. I rated myself around a 7-8 on a scale of 1-10. My clients had rated me a little higher, around an 8-9. My peers had rated me a little lower. My supervisor, however, rated me between a 0-1. The difference between all of the other scores and hers was dramatically different.

Having given out the 360 results, the facilitators immediately dismissed the class for the day, because they didn't want to be around when we got our scores. In my case, I was livid. I was ticked. I could have understood my boss giving me a mix of high and low scores, but all of her ratings were at the bottom and were a distant departure from anyone else's input. There was a clear and obvious gap between her opinion and everyone else's opinion of my performance. I was angry, and I could see what the problem really was, and that problem was her. And I held the data that proved it.

The next day, we were driven to a swamp in the middle of Walt Disney World's vast property and participated in a series of ropes courses. I had experience in facilitating such sessions, so my inclination was to hang back so that the novice ones could learn the lessons. In our first event, we were given a packet with directions and a compass and told to find a pennant at a certain set of coordinates. In my mind's eye, I could sense where that might be. As the team headed out around the lake to find this orange pennant, some ran ahead of our group of 15 in an effort to beat other teams participating in the same activities. "Come on, Kober, help us out." I showed initial reluctance, but, after some cajoling, found myself heading out ahead of the pack to find this pennant.

I came to this one opening, thinking I had found the location. I quickly looked around, but could see no flag. What I did find was a tall beam reaching up into the sky with a sign posted. Still, no pennant. I thought that perhaps I needed to move a little further east. After some 10-15 minutes of doing so, I could hear the rest of the team yelling, "Jeff, where are you? Come back!"

I headed back in the direction I originally came from, only to find the team in the same area I had first arrived at, near the beam that was sitting in the forest clearing. All were busy looking for the pennant, when suddenly, someone reached under some leaves, held up an orange flag, and yelled, "I found it!" Immediately I exclaimed, "That's the first place I looked!"

Hmm.

The facilitator was insightful and took our team under a tree, handed each of us a bottle of water, and debriefed what happened. Some members who had gone ahead mentioned wanting to help the team by finding the pennant, so that when the rest of the team caught up, we would be ahead of the other teams. The facilitator then noted that there was never any mention of this being a competition. That gave energy to others who had come together as a group. They expressed appreciation to those "like Kober" who went ahead to try to find the pennant, but wished everyone had worked together and were frustrated that they really didn't know what those ahead of the pack were doing.

It was a hot day in June with not a cloud in the sky, but you would have thought a lightning bolt came out and hit me. Somehow, I had heard that same commentary being offered to me before.

I don't remember much else of that happened that day. We went back to the classroom later that afternoon and debriefed the experience. Some participants mentioned the importance of working as a T.E.A.M. and that "Together Everyone Achieves More." I listened for a while, and then I shared my thoughts. I mentioned receiving my 360 scores and how my supervisor had rated me. I also noted my anger at her for giving me such low marks. But then, I realized that the same feedback my colleagues had given me in that forest glade was really the same feedback my boss had been trying to give me for some time. She really didn't know what I was up to, and I wasn't being very collaborative in aligning myself with the agenda she was trying to accomplish. Moreover, even though I knew where to look, I would have never found it if I hadn't worked with others. I simply needed to do a better job collaborating.

Before we ended that day, the facilitators gave out an award. Now, if you're like me, you've probably had your share of certificates and trophies over the years. But this one means something different to me, and, in fact, it's the only one I have kept to this day. It was given in honor of the one who best represented the idea of "getting on the bus." And the award? It was a Mickey Mouse school bus lunch box. It was signed by all the Cast Members who were part of that experience that day, and it remains one of my most cherished possessions from my time at Disney.

Now I would like to say it was "happily ever after" with my supervisor after that day. In reality, we still had our ups and downs. But the lesson has remained with me, and I think that it's the most valuable lesson I've taken from my time at Disney. You see, working at Disney isn't about being the next Walt. It's about being a supportive team member. It's about our ability to lead out in collaborating and in creating something greater together. All of my successes since have been due to adhering to that principle. It's the heart of this thing called Team Disney, and it's probably at the heart of any company who ultimately wants to be successful.

By the way, if you ever get around to visiting Disney's Animal Kingdom Lodge, you'll be standing where I stood the day I learned that lesson, in the shadow of that giant post, whose sign read, "Future Front Door of Disney's Animal Kingdom Lodge".

There is wisdom in the airplane safety directive that says, **"Put on your oxygen mask first, before you stop to help others."** That's at the heart of what I learned that one hot day. I needed to fix me before I tried fixing others.

There's another safety adage: "Stop, Drop, & Roll". Only, at the Living Seas, it could be phrased a little differently.

Stop, Drop, and Drain
LEADERS MOBILIZE OTHERS

If you've ever visited the Living Seas at Epcot, you've undoubtedly passed by the diver lock-out chamber, which stands in the center of the exhibit space.

In the late 1990s, we were hosting a Disney Institute customer service program upstairs at the lounge adjacent to Sea Base Alpha. Originally designed for use by United Technologies and their employees, it now serves as a group meeting space. If you have not seen it, it is one of the most beautiful places at Epcot. The lounge is a relaxing room embellished with windows overlooking the aquatic habitat at the Seas.

We spent the morning doing breakfast and some programming and were about to step out into the Seas to do a tour, when we learned what was going on next door. As a matter of procedure, the lock-out chamber is filled and emptied before Guests come in. In the process of doing so, it unexpectedly shattered. Not only did the plexiglass go everywhere, but so did the water, flooding the entire bottom floor of Sea Base Alpha. Fortunately, no one was hurt. But now, Sea Base Alpha was indeed a sea.

In a heartbeat, crews from all over Epcot hastily began moving water out of the building. More wet vacs than you've ever seen in your life were sucking up water in all directions. It was a sight to

145

behold. Clearly, the lock-out chamber was down for good.

The amazing thing was that Sea Base Alpha was completely dried out and the chamber was draped, allowing Guests into the building by noon that day. The turnaround was impressive. **One of the things that Disney does best is bringing all hands on deck when needed.** Cast Members respond quickly and willingly and often sacrifice their own time with little regard to their personal needs.

I refer to this as the ability of an organization to act when matters are urgent and important. One national intelligence agency I worked with was expert at this as well. Any crisis, anywhere, at any time, was handled with great professionalism. But when it came to doing those things that improved the organization over the long haul—things that were important, but not urgent—they struggled.

Our next example comes from next door at Epcot. It illustrates a challenge many organizations face.

A Fountain of Challenges
LEADERS REMOVE SILOS

At The Land Pavilion at Epcot, there was a time in which there was a white sculpted fountain in the center of the atrium. Since Soarin' came in, and a remodel of the restaurant there has taken place, it has been since removed. But for many years it stood as a focal point to The Land, with water running down its semi-circular design.

Back in the 1990s, the newly appointed VP of Epcot, George Kalogridis, came through the Land Pavilion. The executive found the fountain in the center of the building not functioning. He, of course, knew that not having the fountain working was "bad show" to the Guests. He wanted to take action to get it fixed. The fountain was displayed in the food court, so he approached some food & beverage personnel working there at the time. They acknowledged that the fountain was not working, but just because it was in the middle of their seating area didn't make it their responsibility. Inquiring as to whose job it was to fix the fountain, they surmised that it was probably operations—after all, it seemed like they were in charge of most things in the park.

George sought out someone in operations. He explained to them that the fountain wasn't working. They acknowledged that not only was it not working, but that it was probably someone in food & beverage who sent him over to them. After all, everyone thinks it's operation's job. But it wasn't. When George asked whose job it was, they blurted out "Maintenance. If it's broke you should talk to maintenance!" George asked where maintenance was located. They pointed to a small door, and explained that he needed to go down the hallway, make a couple of turns, and then ring the bell when he arrived at the maintenance office.

George stepped through the door, walked down the hallway, made a few turns, and then, entering the maintenance office, rang the bell. Out came a maintenance manager—probably unaware of who the individual was that he was talking to. George explained the problem with the fountain and asked if it was theirs to handle. The answer was affirmative! But then unaware of who the visitor was on the other side of the counter, the individual invited the VP to fill out a job order and they would get around to getting the fountain fixed. As I recall, the maintenance person also asked George to get his supervisor's signature on the form.

I share this story when I teach programs and I ask them if they've ever had this problem before. People are always raising their hands—and not because they have a fountain! **In truth, too often organizations fail because people work in silos**. There are so many challenges inherent when this happens:

- People failing to take ownership
- People expecting others to fix the problem
- Paperwork and red tape established to address the issue

- Details that become unattended until someone in upper management points them out

Additional conversations led George to realize that the operation was working as a grouping of individual silos, each only concerned with their own duties. In time, it was decided to change the organization into business units, with The Land being part of one of a set of such businesses in the park. Each would have a senior manager that would be responsible for the entire operation, including fountains.

George has gone on to manage the park operations in Disneyland Paris, Disneyland, and then finally, Walt Disney World as a whole. I met up with George not long ago as we both waited for planes. I asked if he would have approached it differently if he had to do it again. He said that it really did make sense to him at that time, but also acknowledged that he was currently moving in a very different organizational direction in his present role.

In truth, if there is a time and place to Hard Wire, this might be it. When it works, it does so because you've added training and communications, tools and resources, and support and recognition. It's important to emphasize the need to work collaboratively to accomplish the work of the organization, rather than allowing problems to fall through the cracks.

Can One Imagineer Build Spaceship Earth?
LEADERS LEAD GREAT GROUPS

Imagine only one Imagineer being assigned to build Spaceship Earth at Epcot from the ground up. You could hardly imagine that only one individual could do all of the design, development, and construction. You would need many people to make that kind of dream a reality. For instance, Buckminster Fuller, who we will discuss later, pioneered the concept of a geodesic sphere. But even he himself could not singlehandedly create such an amazing piece of work. We spoke about the "Disney Touch" earlier when it comes to animation. The same could be said for

Imagineering. There are so many hands that touch a project like this, that it's really inappropriate to give credit to a few.

Yet, that's the experience you get when you ride Spaceship Earth. Going through the events of the Renaissance, you see the Sistine Chapel being painted by Michelangelo. Of course, it was Michelangelo's vision that is at the center of that great work, in the same way that it was Buckminster Fuller's vision to create a geodesic sphere. But the truth is that the Sistine Chapel was painted not just by Michelangelo, but also by a crew of nearly a dozen others. And still more were involved in mixing paints, preparing scaffolding, or cleaning brushes.

Look at any number of successful organizations, like Apple, Pixar, or Google, whose great leaders succeeded because they are in a fertile relationship with talented people who collaborate together. As they say, **"None of us is as smart as all of us."** Warren Bennis refers to this as Great Groups. He notes:

> The genius of Great Groups is that they get remarkable people—strong individual achievers—to work together to get results. But these groups serve a second and equally important function: they provide psychic support and personal fellowship. They help generate courage. Without a sounding board for outrageous ideas, without personal encouragement and perspective when we hit a roadblock, we'd all lose our way.

That is the power of influence. It is much greater than one's ability to be in control. It's your ability to create such influence so as to be able to direct a Great Group. And together, that creates excellence. **If Walt Disney had one single strength, it was the gift of bringing together a great group.**

What does this have to do with your organization? Leadership Excellence is not derived by the greatness of one individual. It is derived by the excellence of Great Groups. And a Great Group is comprised of three types of leaders–Positional, Spontaneous, and Personal–just as we mentioned in the first chapter of this book.

Organizations need more leaders (not necessarily more managers) to succeed. The way to create greater leadership is for everyone to focus on building influence.

A Grand Canyon of Leaders
LEADERS EMPLOY GREAT TALENT

Take a few monorails from Epcot and you get to Disney's Contemporary Resort. That's where I was one night, getting a bite to eat, when I was approached by a friendly Cast Member. I was admiring one of the largest artistic pieces found at Walt Disney World, stretching to 90 feet high. It is a stylistic depiction of the Grand Canyon. As I studied the nuances of that great mural, the Cast Member approached me and wanted to share a little bit of Disney insight with me.

"Do you know who created The Grand Canyon mural?"

"Who?" I replied, allowing her to share what she knew.

"Mary Blair!"

"And who else?" I asked.

She looked puzzled. I smiled and took her a few feet around the corner. I then pointed her toward a set of one-foot-square tiles forming a quiet cornerstone.

"All of these artists."

"I didn't know that!" was her surprised response.

It's true. While Mary Blair's artistic style covers the 1800 tiles of this four-sided expression, there are many others who really played a role during the 18 months involved in making this creation a reality.

Perhaps it's Walt Disney who puts it best:

It seems to me shallow and arrogant for any man in these times to claim he is completely self-made, that he owes all his success to his own aided efforts. **Many hands and hearts and minds generally contribute to anyone's notable achievements.**

Leadership & You

As a leader, consider the following:

- How do I get people to align to the same vision?

- How do I get people to abandon individual egos for the pursuit of a dream?

- How do I find the right fit individuals who want to be part of a great group?

- Do I find unity or dissension from responding to an emergency? Are people more intent on pointing blame or taking responsibility?

- What silos exist in my own organization?

- How can I organize and hold each person accountable for collaborating and supporting one another?

- How can I recognize and provide incentives to support those who perform successfully, both in their individual area, as well as in terms of the entire team?

13

LET'S GET TOGETHER
LEADERS KEEP THE SANDBOX FRIENDLY

Let's get together, yeah, yeah, yeah.
Why don't you and I combine?
Let's get together, what do you say?
We can have a swinging time.
We'd be a crazy team.
Why don't we make a scene? Together.
Oh, oh, oh, oh

Let's get together, yeah, yeah, yeah.
Think of all that we could share.
Let's get together, everyday
Every way and everywhere.
And though we haven't got a lot
We could be sharing all we've got. Together.

Those lyrics come from a popular song written by the songwriting team of Robert and Richard Sherman for the 1961 Disney film, *The Parent Trap*. It was sung in the film by Hayley Mills, who starred against herself as she played twin sisters learning to get along with each other.

The song debuted on the Billboard Hot 100 and rose to become a top 10 hit. It propelled the Sherman brothers to other cinematic hits such as *Mary Poppins*.

The lyrics send a fun message about teaming up together. Yet the irony of all this is that the Sherman brothers as successful as they were, really didn't enjoy working together. Moreover, they had no association with each other afterward and their families were practically strangers to one another. Roy E. Disney referred to their temperament as polar opposites: "Bob is 'Feed the Birds,' Dick is 'Supercalifragilisticexpialidocious.'"

It wasn't until 2002, at the London stage premiere of *Chitty Chitty Bang Bang*, that their sons started to reach out to each other. At that time, one brother was living in Beverly Hills and the other in London. Their sons, Gregg and Jeff, began to interview people who knew their fathers over the years. Disney legends, like Julie Andrews, Roy E. Disney, Angela Lansbury, and Dick Van Dyke, all wanted to share their memories of working with the brothers. When Gregg showed his father the emotional interview done with Kenny Loggins, he turned to his son and agreed to get the families together.

The result became *The Boys: The Sherman Brothers' Story*, a movie that makes no villain out of either brother, but simply tries to show how different people work together. While it's ironic that they went so long unable to reconcile personally, it is amazing that what made them come together creatively was their conflict toward each other. That friction created a contribution of an amazing musical library crafted over six decades, far longer than other song-writing greats such as the Beatles or the Beach Boys.

The Spirit of Compromise
LEADERS BUILD THROUGH COMPROMISE

Walt Disney and his brother Roy O. Disney understood the importance of working together as brothers—even though at times they had major fallouts with each other. Once when two department heads quarreled, Roy sent a telegram on December 29, 1942 by overnight wire—declaring, "I don't see why you two can't work together. You are both working for the same company...none of us should have any pride of authorship of ideas but give and take and work with each other amicably. Happy New Year."

Years later, Walt noted: **"Everything here at Disneyland and at the Studio is a team effort."** That was especially difficult, since the studio was made up of artists with individual talents. Putting them together was not always easy. A defining point came after Walt passed away, and while the organization was in the middle of creating The Haunted Mansion.

Every major attraction at Disney goes through years of development before it opens to the public. From idea to opening day, there is a long process in creating a great Guest experience. But few attractions have had a longer development period than The Haunted Mansion, which opened to Guests in October of 1969. Even before Disneyland opened in 1955, there were ideas of an old weathered home at the end of one of the side streets of Main Street, U.S.A. at Disneyland.

Several artists took turns at creating some kind of spook alley-style experience. In time, there formed two frames of thought on the mansion. One group of Imagineers, led by Claude Coats, provided a sort of moody, dark experience. The other group, largely led by Marc Davis, took from his success with Pirates of the Caribbean and a redo on the Jungle Cruise to create a montage of funny experiences. Both groups went back and forth. It came down to scary vs. silly.

Then, matters only became more complicated when Walt passed away in 1966. In the past, Walt would typically break such ties. Now they had to work it out alone.

Tony Baxter, in Jason Surrell's *Haunted Mansion* book, explains that the compromise ended up creating a sort of three-act play–one that enacted the creepiness of Claude Coats in the first third, the comedy of the Davis graveyard scenes in the third part, and a marriage of the two during the ballroom and the attic scenes.

When the Haunted Mansion finally opened, Guest reviews were mixed. Many baby boomers were in their teenage years and were looking for something much scarier. Still, lines were long, and they continue to be today. In many ways, the attraction is timeless because of its mix of creepy and funny.

In the end, the creative compromises that were made on the attraction not only served to make it a better Guest experience, but it has made the attraction both timeless and popular. Sometimes you have to use a little creative compromise. It can be interesting to see where other great ideas can be married to yours.

Plan 67 and Plan 17
LEADERS INVITE FRESH IDEAS TO THE TABLE

There's a great little tale about Rolly Crump in his biography, *It's Kind of a Cute Story*. Rolly was asked by Marty Sklar to create a version of what Epcot would ultimately look like. By this time, many versions had evolved under the direction of John Hench. It had long left the idea of being part of a city, and had evolved into the idea of being a world's fair-type experience. John's designs at this time were largely buildings that were crescent shape in design, not too different from Innoventions today, but still somewhat sterile from an exterior view.

John apparently was caught by considerable surprise when he saw Rolly's version. Part of Rolly's design was to create a World Showcase as a series of islands, each with its own country on it. You would use boats and bridges to move from one pavilion to another. While not practical, it was very much an "out of the box" approach to building Epcot.

Eventually the moment came when both artists saw the work of the other, resulting in a defensive exchange between the two— whose artistic style and vision couldn't have been further apart. John countered that Rolly had no clue about building a theme park. Rolly was so bold as to declare the look of John's project as being a bunch of condos.

Clearly, Marty choosing to involve Rolly was an effort to break up the stale look and feel. I imagine it wasn't too long after this that the World Showcase, and even Future World, started to evolve in a completely different way. Make no doubt about it—the design of the Epcot we enjoy today is John Hench's signature more than anyone else. But he probably wouldn't have reached further and created the "travel around the World Showcase Lagoon" concept we know today, without additional ideas from Rolly and others.

Disney's 1976 annual report shows Marty Sklar, John Hench, and John DeCuir, of what was then WED Enterprises, discussing the key concept at that time, which was merging World Showcase and Future World into one major exposition. This was a major "aha" that saved the company substantial money in only having to build one infrastructure to serve the park rather than two infrastructures for two parks.

In defending the ongoing work, the report went on to say, "This evolutionary creative process is natural to any development of any project at Walt Disney Productions. The report noted: **It was 'Plan 67' which was finally built at Disneyland, and it is 'Plan 17' that you see at Walt Disney World today."**

I would love to know what the number was on Epcot when it was finally built.

There are many projects going on throughout the Disney parks and resorts. Occasionally, a few miss the mark. But by and large, the quality of the work in such projects as Radiator Springs, Mystic Manor, Pandora, and Aulani is truly exciting. Guests respond enthusiastically with their feet and wallets to the quality of great attractions. But the work takes time and investment. It takes time to think out of the box, and sometimes it takes time to break out of the bureaucratic issues that hold back the possibilities of a project.

Pleasure Island Craziness
LEADERS AVOID PITTING OTHERS AGAINST EACH OTHER

That kind of collaboration has not always been sought out. The opposite of collaboration is competition. Michael Eisner thought at times that internal strife was healthy to the organization. For instance, when Pleasure Island opened in 1989 at Walt Disney World, the company wanted to create an experience that would drive revenues from adult-style venues. The created mix of restaurants, dance, and comedy clubs was not something that current management could get their heads around. After months of what Eisner called "hectoring" park executives about making it work, he finally sent his own assistant, Art Levitt, down to Orlando. Art had no experience in tourism, but he was single, thirty years old, and knew how to have a good time. Eisner's mandate to Art: "If I'm not hearing from our park guys that they want to fire you…then you're not screaming loud enough."

To Art's credit, he did put Pleasure Island on the map. By the time he moved on, Pleasure Island was the hip place to be. Chief among his accomplishments was the nightly New Year's Eve celebration. The countdown, accompanied by scantily clad dancers, bands, and enough confetti to wrap the entire complex in a ribbon of paper, worked to bring in crowds. Even Disney's own Cast Members got into it. The place would be flooded on Thursday nights by Cast Members who had just been paid that day. Pleasure Island of the nineties was solid gold.

But at what cost? One unnamed colleague in James B. Stewart's *DisneyWar* noted, **"What Michael [Eisner] likes to do is put six pit bulls together and see which five die."** That competitive versus collaborative approach didn't create an evergreen solution. Despite the glamour of the evening, Pleasure Island would look like a ghost town on hot summer afternoons. The generation that partied hard during that era eventually moved on. In the long run, much of it was mowed down and re-built into what is known today as Disney Springs.

Tokyo Disney's Lighthouse for Consensus
LEADING BY CONSENSUS

Perhaps a better example of an effort toward consensus could be found at the Tokyo Disney Resort. Here you'll find two of perhaps the finest parks ever created—thanks to a partnership between Disney Imagineering and the Oriental Land Company. When you enter Tokyo DisneySea, you are greeted by an amazing water sculpture titled "AquaSphere". It's a symbolic reminder that you are entering a park dedicated to fantastic harbors across the globe.

In their own humble history of their organization, the Oriental Land Company, or OLC, shares a little story about how this sculpture came to be the icon that now greets Guests entering this park. Here's what they share:

> Disney initially suggested the idea of a lighthouse. This is because, for most Americans, a lighthouse is associated with positive images of Homecoming, serving as a beacon of a safe return for adventurous seafarers. But for the Japanese, a lighthouse brings up images of melancholy and loneliness, and so, Oriental Land did not believe this would be an appropriate symbol for a Disney theme park. Because of this inherent difference, both sides struggled to find a point of agreement. However, even in these key cultural issues, the two parties were able to continue a passionate yet constructive dialogue. And ultimately, the parties were able to draw forth a new symbol that showcases the Earth as the 'water planet' befitting a theme park themed to the sea, in what was ultimately called the AquaSphere.

There was also a "much heated discussion" on adding the S.S. Columbia, which can be found docked at American Waterfront. The ship is grand in scale, and was an expensive addition to the park. In this instance, Disney Imagineers won out on the dialogue, and OLC concedes that the ship does much to add to the grandeur and scale of that side of the park.

This is a leadership trait of the Japanese at Tokyo Disney Resort; they work by consensus. The tradition is almost always to debate an idea until there is agreement on it. Then and only then do they take action.

"On Board" Cruising
LEADERS CREATE A CULTURE OF COLLABORATION

While we're on the topic of building ships, here's another great example of people coming together. When *Disney Magic: The Launching of a Dream* was published, John Hemingway spoke of first hearing about the new cruise line through a mutual friend of his, Mike Reininger, of the Disney Institute. It was the kind of vision that brought John back to his childhood days when he first experienced the S.S. United States. The possibilities "struck a nerve" with John, and soon he signed up to be part of the Disney Cruise Line team that unveiled the first Disney cruise ships to the world.

John notes that, previous to working at Disney, he had always "believed a camel to be a horse created by committee." At Disney, he discovered otherwise. He stated:

> In this environment of collaborative creativity, where good ideas had to endure far beyond the honeymoon, there is a need for consensus. The object is not to realize notions that dazzle on impact, but to fashion concepts that are timeless, forever immune to the vicissitudes of fashion, weather, time,67890- and new management teams. After a while, I learned to trust this process. **I watched everyone's 'brilliant' notions reduced to essentials, made to conform to a greater Disney plan and then to evolve as threads in a tapestry. Today, most individual contributions to the Disney Magic are invisible.**
>
> ...Everything accompanying the birth of the Disney Magic has been an adventure. Here is a ship singular in every

way. It defies convention and, in the end, it is the collective dream of many.

Again, The Disney Touch.

Many people quickly associate the phrase "Death by Committee" to the work most committees do. And at Disney, there are many movies and attractions that are testimony to the failure of a committee. Disney California Adventure in its original form, through the hosting of a design charrette, and other committee meetings, is believed to be a powerfully expensive example of how something may fail when it is left in the hands of committees.

Still, there is power in consensus and in councils. Even Walt Disney, with the singleness of vision that he brought to the company, relied on committees, especially in the latter years when there were too many projects for him to be attentive to all the details. The problem is that too often committees fail to follow the rules that allow them to be successful.

Leadership & You

As a leader, consider the following:

- How do I work to reach consensus as a team?

- Do I use competition as a tool for pitting people against each other?

- Am I patient awaiting the outcome while everyone comes together?

- Can I obtain a greater outcome when we work it through until there is a consensus?

- Do I lead for consensus?

- Have I been part of a successful committee? If so, why was it successful?

- Have I been part of a dysfunctional committee? If so, what did I learn about that?

- If I could build a dream team to help make my visions come true, what characteristics would I look for?

14

LISTEN WITH YOUR HEART
LEADERS COMMUNICATE

It's what Pocahontas says to John Smith, as she invites him to understand the world around him: "Listen with your heart, you will understand."

This timeless message is not just about understanding nature. It is also about understanding people who are different from you. She explains: "You think the only people who are people are the people who look and think like you. But if you walk the footsteps of a stranger, you'll learn things you never knew you never knew."

Understanding others, learning tolerance, and gaining empathy allows us to better approach the conflicts we have with others. This chapter explores that approach.

Hanging Together Under the Liberty Tree
LEADERS TAKE TIME TO INFORMALLY LISTEN TO OTHERS

Turn the pages of history to a later colonial period, and you step into a setting similar to what one finds in Liberty Square at the Magic Kingdom. Here in this plaza, you find shade and rest under the Liberty Tree. This tree represents a famous elm tree that stood in Boston, near Boston Common, in the days before the American Revolution. The tree was a rallying point for the growing resistance to the rule of England over the American colonies. It is considered by some to be the site "where America was born." In time, such trees were designated throughout other towns.

In those times, holding an unauthorized assembly or meeting was dangerous business that carried threats of imprisonment or death by British troops. The casual appearance of a group chatting beneath a tree was much safer. As resistance to the laws of England became greater, colonists would gather to determine how to resist the suppression. There they would assemble, express views, and vent emotions. **The lanterns on the Liberty Tree suggest that as colonists they must come together.**

Such a place exists in offices today. It's known as a water cooler. Water coolers are really unofficial gathering places. In morning meet-ups, employees meander over to the coffee pot and kibitz. At noon, you might see them sitting around the office kitchen. Later in the afternoon, it's off to the water cooler. Even Walt noticed this when he said, "As you can see, we have our most important conferences around the water cooler."

To a manager, many of these kinds of activities are a waste of time. But directed appropriately, these activities serve to do the following:

First, they create a social network where people feel connected to one another.

Second, it allows employees to talk out feelings, hopes, and frustrations, all of which serve to help them feel heard and understood.

Third, it creates a sense of collaboration and unity in doing the work.

With Twitter and other social media sites becoming so prevalent, many of those liberty trees and water coolers are becoming virtual. Either way, the solution is for leaders to hang their lantern under the tree with the rest of them. It's not enough to have an open door policy. By taking time to socialize in informal ways, you can create a greater corporate culture. Foster positive networking and communication and reap the harvest of a more unified organization.

Of course, even the best efforts to create an interchange with others can result in an eventual conflict. How you deal with the one in such conflicts sends a huge message to the ninety and nine.

Monsters, In Communication
LEADERS KEEP CHANNELS OF COMMUNICATION OPEN

Over the course of a few years, Pixar grew from a small organization to a major studio working on multiple films at one time. Knowing who is doing what and being clear about priorities can become as confusing in animation as it is in any major organization. One of the challenges organizations face is that management, in an effort to feel like things are under control, will often control the communication process.

Of leading Pixar, Ed Catmull noted:

> **We had made the mistake of confusing the communication structure with the organizational structure.** Of course an animator should be able to talk to a modeler directly, without first talking with his or her manager. So we gathered the company together and said: Going forward, anyone should be able to talk to anyone else, at any level, at any time, without fear or reprimand. Communication would no longer have to go through hierarchical channels.

This challenge happens throughout any organization, and it especially happens at Disney. Disney has come up with many a creative approach to its organizational structure. But at the end of the day, what's necessary is that the culture be flat enough for people to talk to whomever they need to in order to get the job done.

20,000 Leagues of Disagreement
LEADERS AGREE TO DISAGREE

Listening with your heart also requires a willingness to agree to disagree. It requires creating a greater tolerance for opinions that are contrary to yours. Dick Nunis shares this experience about a Disneyland steering committee meeting he attended:

> I was giving this pitch to Walt and he was just killing me. He said, "Nunis, you don't know what you're talking about," and walked out of the room. Everybody followed him and I sat there in this big room all by myself. I thought I had been fired and was thinking of where I would go to get a new job when I heard the door open behind me. It was Walt. He put his hand on my shoulder and said, **"Look, young fella, you keep expressing your opinions; I like it."**
>
> I think he tested people. Later I would sit in meetings and watch him take a position and see who would go with him. Then he would take the opposite position and see who would go with him. I think the people who stuck to their guns, whether they were right or wrong, were the people he respected the most.

The table of that lesson would turn. After Walt Disney World opened, lines for the submarine voyage, 20,000 Leagues Under the Sea, had grown long and slow. A discussion was being held regarding whether or not to build a second dock and add more subs, at a cost of millions of dollars. A young Bruce Laval, whose assignment was to create some serious measurements revolving around how Guests moved throughout the park, opposed Dick Nunis and contended that once the somewhat-adjacent Space Mountain opened (it was under construction), the wait times for 20,000 Leagues would go down. Dick countered that argument, saying that when Haunted Mansion opened up at Disneyland, the thought was that the lines at Pirates of the Caribbean next door would go down. Instead, they increased.

Bruce countered again by saying the problem was that to justify a ticket price increase, Disneyland had added an extra "E ticket" to the ticket books. On a peak day, that was creating an additional 60,000 E tickets, resulting in great demand to use that ticket on Pirates.

When Bruce Laval was finished, the room grew silent. Dick stated, "Well…that all sounds good, but that's just not the way it will work." Bruce noted that there would be no additional E tickets when Space Mountain opened, so there would be one less E ticket to use. It was simple supply and demand economics.

Finally, Nunis stated, "Well, young man, you sound awfully confident don't you?" Laval said, "Yes sir I am, and I will bet my job on it." In an even sterner voice Dick replied, "We don't bet jobs here—we only bet money." With tension in the room, Bruce spoke up and said, "Well then I will bet my salary against your salary." Everyone suddenly erupted into laughter, breaking the tension.

And the additional dock for 20,000 Leagues? Ultimately, it was never needed as crowds mobbed the new Space Mountain.

Tangled with Feedback
LEADERS BUILD OTHERS THROUGH FEEDBACK

As managers, our words can have a powerful effect, positive or negative, on the morale of others. I was on the Disney Magic enjoying a week of vacation with my family. The cruise did not disappoint–as a cruise ship, the Disney Magic is Magical! But I had one particular experience that really stood out. One of the most magical experiences was the new *Tangled* show.

Afterward, we stayed in our seats chatting about what we loved most about the show. By the time we moved toward the lobby, we were among the last few to leave the theater. At the exit to the theater, Crew Members had assembled with a big yellow trash can and several brooms, ready to clean up for the later showing. As I passed by, Clayton Lyndsey, serving as Cruise Director for the Disney Magic, came running up to these Crew Members and gently urged them to return the trash receptacle and brooms back into the closet until *every* Guest had left the theater.

He got it!

Clayton understood that the company had spent millions upon millions to build the most beautiful ship, had created a fantastic show, and the Guests were leaving with the last part of that experience being the scene of yellow trash cans and brooms. He understood that you can't spend so much time creating magic, only to let it go at the end.

But more importantly, **he knew that the Crew Members trying to do their job didn't need some scolding or put down, they just needed some careful feedback and coaching.** The experience played out similarly to the one Imagineer John Hench shares about Walt Disney in his book, *Designing Disney: Imagineering and the Art of the Show.*

> Walt was also keen to make dining a good experience for Guests, not just a necessity. He would walk the park in disguise, wearing an old hat and dark glasses, observing how people were treated. On one of these walks, I saw him stop at the newly opened restaurant, Plaza Pavilion, with table seating outside.
>
> A young boy was bussing dishes, scraping them into a cardboard box at the table in front of the diners—not a very appetizing thing to watch. Walt walked over to the boy, patiently and quietly explained to him that cleaning plates should not be exposed to the Guests, and asked the boy to take the used dishes back to the kitchen to clean them. Walt waved his hand a bit; the boy nodded, and removed the dishes. I watched the whole thing from a distance. I keep seeing this picture in my mind; I was really shocked by the whole thing. It did look bad from the Guests' point of view, but Walt didn't raise hell with the busboy's boss; he spoke only to the boy. I am sure that neither the boy

nor the diners knew that it was Walt. It was typical of Walt to go to the source of the problem in this way.

I felt Clayton Lyndsey did the same in his experience on the Disney Magic. He stepped forward as a leader, re-directing the well-intentioned efforts of the crew until all of the Guests had departed. He didn't make a big thing about it. He didn't involve their boss. He just explained to the Crew Members that you don't want to break the magic!

Walt wasn't always so gentle with others. Sometimes in his impatience, he could measure out an "eye for an eye" type of treatment to individuals he felt were being boorish or difficult. But conversely, he was aware of his own conduct with those who might be overwhelmed by that kind of direct response. Claude Coats, who Walt knew for years, was known as a "gentle giant" of a guy. His wife noted: "Walt was always nice to Claude…He knew that Claude was sensitive. Instead of putting down something Claude was doing, he'd suggest an alternative."

Communication works when alternatives are given in the right manner. Let's explore some options for doing so.

A Castle Tower of "Yes...If"
LEADERS BUILD ON THE IDEAS OF OTHERS

It matters not only how we communicate up and down the chain of command, but also how we speak with our peers. Imagineer Tom Morris began his career as a balloon seller at Disneyland as a teenager. He graduated from position to position until he became the designer of Fantasyland for Disneyland Paris at the time of its construction. In the book, *One Little Spark*, by Marty Sklar, Tom shares an experience between Marty and Eddie Sotto, who was responsible for the design of Main Street, U.S.A.

> I call it Additive Collaboration. It's not enough to say simply collaborate, for you could do that by holding your nose and grudgingly going with the flow because you were

told to, or because there's no other choice. Buzz Price (economic adviser to Walt Disney and former chairman of CalArts) spoke often about 'yes IF' enablement, and improvisational theater has long taught us the importance of "yes AND". **That is what addictive collaboration is about: not being afraid to make someone else's idea work or to enhance an idea of your own by incorporating others' ideas and designs into it.**

A personal example is what happened to me when I was directing the design of the castle for Disneyland Paris. After personally completing the design for the main tower, about which I was very self-congratulatory, I showed it to my colleague Ed Sotto, who was directing the creative efforts for Main Street, just to get feedback (and, really, to only hear "great job" and nothing else). His feedback was "Looks great, but have you considered making the arches under the balcony look like tree branches?" (This was a motif being used elsewhere on the castle).

It would have been easy to say "yes, but" or "no, this" (or "mine, mine..."), but I had to admit it was a great idea and immediately incorporated it...because it was the best thing for the overall design and Guest experience.

The concept of Additive Collaboration that Tom Morris references in his story is important. When concepts and ideas are intertwined, they become stronger than if they were branches unto themselves. You've heard those kinds of statement that are like branches that go nowhere. Statements like:

- "That won't work here because..."
- "We've already tried that before."
- "We're not like that/them."
- "That's not how we do things here."
- "Been there...done that."

These statements have been a hallmark of many a negative, cynical conversation. To truly collaborate, you must be open to all ideas; not that all will survive, but those ideas require nurturing to truly see their potential. Making that happen must be intentional, however, and not simply left to nature and fate. Tom mentions two great tools that lead to that.

The first statement is "Yes...if". Rather than saying "Yes...but", the statement **"Yes...if" suggests that do-ability of accomplishing something if we can then make the right circumstances occur.** That re-focuses the conversation to how to make it happen, rather than whether it can happen.

"Yes...and" is tremendous at putting down the defensiveness that arises out of competitive ideas in a conversation. **"Yes...and" allows you to build upon an idea, rather than tear it down and build from scratch.**

Can you create through additive collaboration? It may require leaving your pride at the door. But the possibility of listening with your heart requires you being open to others. Alone we can do so little; together we can do so much. Add "Yes...if" and "Yes...and" to your toolkit for building a more collaborative experience.

Leadership & You

As a leader, consider the following:

- How am I creating a place where people can gather and share ideas freely?

- What are ways I can easily break the magic in our social interactions with others?

- Can I agree to disagree?

- How do I handle it in a way that puts things back on track, and doesn't make a mountain out of a molehill?

- Do I utilize "Yes...but" or Yes...and" in my conversations?

- Does my feedback build and edify, or hurt and tear apart?

- What kind of relationship do I need so that people will accept my feedback?

- What would additive collaboration look like in my organization?

15

WINDOWS ON MAIN STREET
LEADERS RECOGNIZE OTHERS

In consulting with organizations, we often highlight the importance of reward and recognition to the culture. Disney has been doing this for many years in a variety of ways. Here's a look at how this is important at Disney.

Walt Disney's Approach to Recognition
LEADERS CARVE OUT THEIR OWN APPROACH TO RECOGNITION

There is no more confusing aspect of Walt Disney's behavior than his attitude toward employee recognition. For all of his strengths, for all that he managed to do, perhaps the one place where he fell short was in recognizing the work of others—at least the way we think of doing so. Simply saying "thanks" was the exception, not the norm. Typically, "that will do" was the ultimate verbal response from him. In today's society where we speak of giving employees praise and recognition, it seems odd at least that he wasn't more effusive in his praise.

It may have been how he was raised by his parents—perhaps it was his own Midwestern roots. But for whatever reason, Walt seemed to lack the ability to praise others. Not that there weren't moments or evidence of this. Bill Cottrell, the first president of what would become Imagineering recalled: "In the earlier days of the studio, Walt used to come to the shop and if they were building a beautiful piece of furniture, he'd say, 'Who did this?

He'd say, 'Gee that's beautiful, how do you turn this?' He was interested in knowing how to do it. He eventually had a shop of his own. You'd be surprised at how much that did for morale. To have someone come in and say, 'That's beautiful.' That didn't happen after a while."

On occasion, Walt Disney wouldn't give the positive feedback directly to the individual. But he would talk up how amazing that individual was to others. Staff members quickly then disseminated to that employee or artist what Walt had mentioned to them. This form of triangulation worked only because it was Walt's way of making you stand out among others.

Bill offers no insight as to why such forms of recognition "didn't happen after a while." Keep in mind that Walt didn't really like recognition much himself. When one studio staff member took the time to thank him for a particular raise, Walt felt awkward. He simply didn't have the time for a pat on the back. His focus was on moving forward.

What Walt used as recognition, however, was the opportunity to work on projects that were unique and truly amazing. Remember that working on a fresh new project was, for many artists at the studio, a tantalizing notion. Much of the work of animation was simply the precise and rote work of one drawing followed by another. To do something newer, something different that exposed your own artistic self was a gift. To be asked to play a bigger part in brainstorming new ideas was reward in and of itself. Utilizing your artistic form to define the creative work of a film was high praise in and of itself. And being moved from animation to Imagineering where your creative work was brought to life was perhaps the frosting on the cake.

Beyond this, however, there was something about working with Walt Disney that was simply an honor in and of itself. Herb Ryman noted: "There was just something about him that made you want to please him…and gaining his confidence was better than payday."

Regardless of Walt's own personal approach, the company he founded has responded strongly in their acknowledgement of the work its employees provide. Here are examples—formal and informal—of how The Walt Disney Company provides recognition. Let's begin with its highest honors.

Disney Windows and Legends
LEADERS FORMALLY RECOGNIZE OTHERS

The Disney Legends Award is the highest honorary acclaim given to outstanding individuals who have contributed in some way to any segment of the Walt Disney Company. This is not limited to just part of the organization, but to the entire corporation. Still, many of the most important leaders and pioneers who shaped places like Walt Disney World and the rest of the park and resorts division are memorialized as Disney Legends. Comparable to a lifetime achievement award, these individuals are usually presented their awards during the D23 Expo. Like footprints at Grauman's Chinese Theatre, Disney Legends are memorialized with their handprints.

Those handprints are bronzed and then displayed in the Disney Legends Plaza at the Walt Disney Studios in Burbank, California. Each recipient also receives a small Disney Legends Award statue. That award has symbolism to it:

- The Spiral stands for imagination and the power of an idea.

- The Hand holds the gifts of skill, discipline, and craftsmanship.

- The Wand and Star represent magic: the spark that is ignited when imagination and skill combine to create a new dream.

You can see a larger version of this when you visit Disneyland Paris. It resides in the Fantasia Gardens at the entrance to the park. In particular, it recognizes artists and contributors whose origins and roots were in Europe.

Receiving a window on Main Street is a lifetime achievement award for those who contributed in some pioneering way to the Disney parks, though early leaders across the Disney organization are also memorialized, as the Disney Legends award did not come into play until 1987. Corporate leadership determines those honored and only extends this award to individuals who have retired. Their window treatment typically appears as a fictitious business and often refers to their role or some hobby of theirs. Often there is some form of humor or "inside joke" known to the recipient and those close associates.

Some individuals were in managerial executive positions. Others played a more spontaneous or positional role. Still, all were leaders in some way, as we described at the start of this book.

Windows on Main Street are probably the most well-known of all the forms of Disney recognition, but others exist as well. Let's take a look at other creative tributes you can find throughout Walt Disney World.

Some who provide outstanding contributions to the work of the organization are recognized in other unique ways throughout the parks. For example, Harper Goff contributed greatly to the design of many of the original attractions at Disneyland and Walt Disney World. A major nod is given to him at "Harper's Mill" at the curve of the Rivers of America.

Goff actually has several tributes for his work throughout the parks. For instance, he also designed the famed submarine for the film *20,000 Leagues Under the Sea*. So, when a building went up in the location of where that attraction once was at Walt Disney World, it seemed appropriate to again acknowledge him with a reference on a nearby building. The submarine he designed was cleverly etched into the rockwork becoming its own "hidden Mickey".

Many of these tributes largely feature Disney Imagineers but not all. In Bonjour Gifts in Fantasyland, you see a portrait of Phil Holmes, who served as the head of Magic Kingdom for many years. Surrounding his image are any number of symbols known to those are familiar with all things Disney, such as peanuts from *Dumbo*, and a lamp from *Aladdin*.

Then there's the most macabre recognition of all–tombstones at the Haunted Mansion in the Magic Kingdom. They honor a number of Imagineers who played a role with that attraction. Again, there is a sort of playfulness. Remember Marc Davis & Claude Coats, mentioned earlier for their contribution? Marc's states: "In Memory of Our Patriarch, Dear Departed Grandpa Marc". Claude's reads: "At Peaceful Rest Lies Brother Claude, Planted Here Beneath This Sod". Of interest to the earlier story, their "plots" reside at opposite ends of the graveyard.

Partners in Excellence
LEADERS ALLOW OTHERS TO RECOGNIZE EXCELLENCE

Most of the forms of recognition noted so far are for senior, lifetime contributors. But what about current Cast Members throughout the Disney parks? The highest honor to any Disney Cast Member is the Disney Legacy Award. It culminates in an annual award ceremony where peers recognize the best of the best within Parks, Cruise Line, and Imagineering. It's only for the organization's best performers. For example, from some 6,000 nominations worldwide, only 650 recipients received the award one year.

Those who receive this award are first honored when their names are announced in individual team meetings or in some personalized way. Later on, they take part in a big evening celebration to mark the occasion where they receive a special commemorative plaque. They also receive a blue nametag distinguishing them from others, which you will see when you are out in the parks.

Note that this recognition effort is a descendant of Partners in Excellence, an earlier reward system that recognized people based on a balanced scorecard performance in three areas:

1. Providing great customer service

2. Supporting and engaging fellow employees

3. Helping to lower and reduce costs

Partners in Excellence was born from the idea that the organization should recognize performance over simply celebrating the anniversary of someone who perhaps should have been gone years prior.

Like the Disney Legacy Award, recipients were nominated by their peers. They received a big celebration, and took home a Partners statue–the same kind you see above in the Legacy Plaza at the corporate headquarters. They also received a pin of the same image to place on their nametag.

The challenge with Partners in Excellence is that it was originally determined that you could only receive the award once. Over time, they ran out of people meeting the criteria to be honored, thus they changed the once only rule, giving it to people who had received it already. And, after a time or two of that, who wants the same award? So they created a new award–one that was more across the entire theme park operation, and not just Walt Disney World. And that's how the Disney Legacy Award came about.

Applause-O-Grams and More
LEADERS RECOGNIZE IN THE MOMENT

Most of the rewards mentioned so far are more formal in nature. What about day-to-day recognition? What about more informal tools? Recognize Now! is an online tool that has been operating in recent years, with one million thank-you messages sent over its first three years. This electronic tool includes leader-reporting features. There are a few ways to recognize others:

Four Keys Card. This recognition is automatically posted to the record card of the Cast Member and is shared with their work area to be included in a monthly drawing. The Four Keys are the primary Guest service standards, and include Safety, Courtesy, Show, and Efficiency.

Instant Appreciation. This is a personalized "Instant Appreciation" message. This is not tied directly to the Four Keys, but is simply a vehicle for saying thanks to others for going out of their way in helping someone.

We should mention that there is a sort of mascot and logo for this program: Russell and his Grape Soda Bottlecap Pin from the Pixar film, *Up*.

This online tool replaced older paper tools, such as the following:

Applause-O-Grams. Recognition to thank Cast Members who went above and beyond in their daily tasks. They could be nominated by Cast Members or by Guests. It utilized an Applause-O-Gram certificate.

Guest Service Fanatic Awards. This was on-the-spot recognition for non-salaried on-stage and backstage Cast Members who consistently delivered great service. You filled out a card, and then dropped it into a box for a monthly drawing.

Excellence Awards. Spot awards to recognize and reward individuals and teams for outstanding contributions while demonstrating excellence. This often included a monetary award.

What sets the Recognize Now! program apart from those just listed is that it's online, and allows those giving the reward to not only customize the certificate/card to the individual, but to place notice of that recognition permanently in the file of the individual. That practice was done before as well, but not as consistently.

And the Oscar Goes To...
LEADERS FIND A VARIETY OF WAYS TO RECOGNIZE AND CELEBRATE

Additionally, there are a few other awards based on specific achievement. Here are examples:

R.A.V.E. Awards. These awards are presented annually to areas that have demonstrated outstanding commitment to achieving excellence in diversity by respecting, appreciating, and valuing everyone. Individuals and areas are honored at an annual luncheon.

Environmentality Champions. This award honors Cast Members who demonstrate outstanding efforts in recycling, waste minimization, and conservation. These are done at the local level, and then are tiered up to the resort-wide level. The award for the champions is made of recycled materials. They receive a $2,500 grant on their behalf to a conservation organization of their choice.

Individual Awards. Beyond this are any number of area awards. These are generally more informal and customized to the specific area. Individual teams can identify their own awards, as can entire operations such as a resort or theme park. For instance, the Magic Kingdom honors Cast Members taking the extra time to be safe by giving them a safety cone. The Traveling Safety Cone is simply a small, decorated safety cone and the Cast Member gets to have their picture taken with it. It's simple and fun, but still emphasizes behaviors that are important to the organization's success.

Earning Outside Awards. Recognition should not only be internal within the organization, but it should take advantage of those honors bestowed from outside organizations and associations. Disney likes to be on the receiving end of those rewards as well. **From the Oscars to the Tony Awards, from Michelin to Conde Nast, these awards are a big thing for Disney. But so are lesser-known acknowledgements from human resource groups or conservation causes.**

Sometimes those moments of recognition come by surprise. But many times, they are the culmination of an effort made by different segments of the organization. Still, they mean something to the teams and individuals who contributed to making them happen.

There are a couple of important messages that can be learned about recognition:

Offer Formal & Informal. There should be both formal and informal ways to recognize others. Many organizations have one or the other, but not both. Organizations with only formal awards end up going too long before getting around to the formal award. Employees receiving only informal thanks find that it becomes rote after awhile.

Make it 360. This means that there should be vehicles for those on the outside to recognize others. There should be a manner in which customers can recognize employees. Peers should have a mode for providing recognition. Finally, supervisors should be able to recognize—and they should be recognized as well!

Provide Symbols of Recognition. The most important part of these is that relatively little cost is usually involved in the actual recognition. Few of these involve some monetary award. That's not to say there aren't Cast Members who receive bonuses. But they alone are not enough to justify someone sacrificing 40 plus years to the Walt Disney World Company. A window on Main Street however, is something that immortalizes you.

Advancement at the Mouse Factory
LEADERS RECOGNIZE THROUGH OPPORTUNITY & PROMOTION

Let's return to the original kind of recognition that Walt Disney would offer—opportunity! A great form of employee engagement is to receive promotions and be given the opportunity to do new things. For many artists at the Disney Studios, that led to new opportunities to direct shorts and feature animation. But it also led many to new opportunities outside of the day-to-day animation focus. Ward Kimball, an animator who always made animated characters come to life in memorable ways, went on to direct a number of television shows, including the *Man in Space* series and *The Mouse Factory*. With the former project, Walt knew that Ward could take scientific concepts and make them entertaining.

The same has occurred in Disney's own park operations. Dick Nunis started with the Disney University, and eventually headed up all of the Disney theme park attractions worldwide. Phil Holmes started as a host at the Haunted Mansion, but eventually went on to be head of Magic Kingdom and after that, Disney's Hollywood Studios. George Kalogridis began by bussing tables at Disney's Contemporary Resort. He would go on to eventually head up the entire Walt Disney World Resort. This is just the tip of the iceberg of people who have made entire careers at Disney, and it's a key component of how people are rewarded and recognized.

Guido Quaroni, whose supervisory role has been associated with software and hardware development, spends a lot of time thinking how to keep 120 engineers happy at Pixar. Remember that engineering is not the focus of Pixar—animation is. So it's not as easy in that role to point to a scene in a movie and feel that you really crafted that moment in the film. But to award his employees, he instituted "personal project days" in his department. Two days a month, he allows his engineers the opportunity to work on any project they feel is important. Pixar's resources are made available to support them in addressing whatever production issue they feel is important. As Guido stated, **"You just give people the time, and they come up with the ideas...That's the beauty of it: It comes from them."** And the result? Those personal project days have done much to engage his employees as well as to move the science of animation forward.

All these ideas are probably more at the heart of where Walt was all along. He felt that perhaps opportunities to do new things was more important than a pat on the back. In truth, everyone likes to be recognized in different ways. Find out what it is, and use it as an incentive for creating excellence.

Here's a simple way of translating all of this. My business partner, Mark David Jones, spoke often in his role at Disney about the notion of identifying the kind of recognition each of his employees liked, and then providing that platinum kind of recognition— where people are treated the way they want to be treated, not the way we think they might like to be treated. He would keep an index card of incentives tailored for each Cast Member. And he'd pull that card out and grab an idea when he wanted to recognize, reward, or celebrate.

Leadership & You

As a leader, consider the following:

- What is recognition like in my organization? How is it unique to my culture?

- Do I have both formal and informal reward and recognition programs implemented?

- Are my programs 360–meaning that there is a vehicle for anyone (employees, supervisors, customers, etc.) to recognize others?

- Do I tie reward & recognition to performance–or to what matters most in the organization?

- Do I align the reward and recognition to my brand and culture?

- Do I focus on symbols of excellence rather than on monetary rewards?

- Do I make recognition fun?

16

JUST A SPOONFUL OF SUGAR
LEADERS MAKE WORK FUN

AN ELEMENT OF FUN
LEADERS STAY POSITIVE DESPITE CIRCUMSTANCES

"In every job that must be done, there is an element of fun. You find the fun and snap! The job's a game. And every task you undertake becomes a piece of cake. A lark! A spree! It's very clear to see that a spoonful of sugar helps the medicine go down." This quotation from *Mary Poppins* is not just the lyrics to a song; it's a philosophy of making the best of everything you do. It's creating the joy despite the hardship. It's an approach Disney has sought to take throughout its history. Roy O. Disney once wrote to his parents:

> While we are not making money hand over fist as the general public thinks, still we are making some money. However, it is all going back into our business. Just think, there are about 130 or 135 people around here, living on Mickey Mouse. He's a pretty good mouse, don't you think, to keep up so many families? Well, we are not particularly concerned whether we ever make millions or not. **After all, what you get in this life is what you take out of it in the way of pleasure, fun, enjoyment, and accomplishment.** I have made up my mind that I am not going to let this thing get me down just for the sake of some money, and I know that Walt feels the same way about it.

By the way, that's what Roy O. Disney wrote in 1933, during the height of the depression, and well before they had their first blockbuster success with *Snow White and the Seven Dwarfs*.

HOW EARLY IS THE MEETING?
LEADERS DON'T TAKE THEMSELVES TOO SERIOUSLY

Everyone agrees that work should be fun, but making it so is not easy—even at the House of the Mouse.

Under the crush of deadlines prior to the opening of Walt Disney World, Dick Nunis had left his family in California and had moved into a cottage in Bay Hill. He often found himself sleeping on a cot in his office. David Koenig, in his book, *Realityland*, noted that every morning, the Disney World Operating Committee would meet in a construction trailer. As deadlines neared, the meetings were scheduled earlier and earlier, until one was set for 6:00 a.m. When Dick arrived the next day, he found his entire committee in bathrobes. Merchandising manager Jack Olsen even had shaving cream on his face.

Dick got the message sent in a fun, kidding way. The meetings went back to a 7:00 am start time.

It's often bureaucracy or office politics that take the fun out of anything and everything. I experienced that for myself.

BARCODE THIS...
LEADERS KEEP A SENSE OF HUMOR ABOUT THE BUREAUCRACY

During my time with the Disney Institute, they wanted to move away from using slide carousels in the classroom. It was simply archaic for the mid-nineties. One of my roles was to devise a better approach. The answer was simply to issue laptops to each facilitator, and to utilize PowerPoint presentations. I met immediate pushback. Senior management didn't trust the facilitators to not lose the laptops.

The temporary answer, until management could see the benefit of laptops, was to use laser discs. In a permanent classroom environment, laser discs actually made sense. Before digital improvements, laser discs offered the best images. They also made it easy to jump from one image or video to another—something much more difficult with VHS tapes. You could place barcodes into the facilitator guides, wave an infrared wand at them, and the image you were looking for immediately came to the screen.

The problem was taking a laser disc machine on the road. These were sensitive electronic products and facilitators often had to go from one city to another. Carrying them required traveling carefully, insulating them from getting bumped around. For the facilitators the equipment was not travel friendly. With that hassle came resentment. Their feedback to me: "Barcode this, Jeff...along with some frustrated expletive." It was all in humor and we often laughed about it. They knew I was the champion for moving to laptops. For several years, the expression "Barcode this!" became the one-liner for whatever was going wrong at any given moment.

As a side note, the case for replacing the screen in our classrooms with monitors and laser discs had been an elaborate process. That involved getting buy-in from Walt Disney World's top architect, Wing T. Chow. As the Executive Vice President in charge of Master Planning, Architecture and Design at Walt Disney Imagineering, Mr. Chow seemed like his time might be better spent on larger issues. Soon, any mention of the bureaucratic process was followed by our singing, "Everybody Wing Chow tonight" referencing the "Everybody Have Fun Tonight" by the British new wave group Wang Chung. It was our little way of having fun in the midst of mind-numbing bureaucracy.

EMPTY MAGIC
LEADERS CREATE A SPACE FOR FUN

Leaders must not only be fun, they must create an environment that welcomes such. When Pixar was purchased, John Lasseter and Ed Catmull, Pixar's top leadership, took over the fledgling animation department at Disney. Prior to the purchase, Disney animation had gone through a difficult, humiliating period with product that did not inspire. John and Ed wanted the Disney Animation Department to come alive with its own culture. After the announcement of Ed's appointment was made, he came to visit the Disney Studios, a beautiful facility with a sorcerer's hat in the front, reminiscent of Mickey's role as the Sorcerer's Apprentice from *Fantasia*.

Since his schedule was busy that day, he took time to tour the facility early in the morning before employees arrived. After walking through several floors, it became apparent that every workspace was not only clean, but there was nothing on it that suggested something about the employee that worked there. No family photos, no tchotchkes, no personal belongings. He asked why, but the host was initially hesitant to reply. Finally, Ed insisted on an answer to his question. The host acknowledged that because new management was coming on board, everyone was told to remove their personal belongings in order to make it look clean and tidy for the visit. This requirement sent a message to Ed about what the culture had deteriorated into. He knew he had to make changes, not in some policy or procedure, but to the culture itself. Those cultural changes eventually would yield to Disney animation creating some phenomenal films, to include *Wreck It Ralph*, *Tangled*, and *Frozen*.

In short, you can't create fun and magic if you don't have a fun, magical place to work in.

VOLUNTEAR FOR FUN
LEADERS ORCHESTRATE OPPORTUNITIES TO HAVE FUN

If you're going to have a fun place to work, you have to be intentional about doing so. While it may happen on its own, it usually requires some kind of orchestration to create the environment for it.

A long standing Disney tradition is a commitment to a friendly and informal work environment. This involves promoting fellowship and camaraderie among the Cast Members as well as their families. We mentioned the softball fields and the Walt Disney Studios and the annual Canoe Races of the World (C.R.O.W.). Of course, Disney Cast Members have access to the theme parks, along with discounts to the cruise lines and resorts. Still, there is much more. Here are some others:

Goofy's Mystery Tour. Take bungee-like cords and tie a team together. Then let them work together to find clues and solve puzzles in the middle of Disney's Hollywood Studios at midnight. Award prizes. That's Goofy's Mystery Tour.

Mickey's Retreat. 19 acres of pools, playgrounds, sports fields and recreational facilities designed not just for employees to enjoy, but their families as well.

Sports Leagues. Basketball, soccer, volleyball, and soccer leagues, played on Disney-owned fields within onstage and backstage areas.

Social Clubs. Opportunities for people to associate based on interest, whether that is Toastmasters, theater groups, fishing teams, or even amateur radio.

Disney VoluntEars. Since 2012, Cast Members have contributed over 3.4 million hours to the communities they are a part of. Their goal is to contribute 5 million hours by 2020.

WHERE TINKER BELL PLAYS BASKETBALL
LEADERS FIND INFORMAL WAYS TO CREATE FUN

It's not just enough to have set programs and events in place for creating an engaged, fun place to work. It needs to come informally as well. Here are some examples:

Few know that within the icy caverns of the mighty Matterhorn at

Disneyland, there was once an actual basketball court. Its establishment was fairly unorganized. This wasn't in the original blueprints. It was the result of attraction personnel and Matterhorn climbers coming together on breaks or between climbs to play games. The court sat high above both the infamous bobsled attraction and where the skyway had once passed through, so Guests never saw it. And it was only a few feet away from Tinker Bell's dressing room, so there was time for her to play before descending down the Matterhorn during the fireworks.

It's not the first time anyone put up a basketball hoop at work, though it is one of the more unusual locations for one. There have been other courts backstage around the parks. Backstage behind River Country comes in mind. A leftover pinball machine from the Penny Arcade could be found in the break room below Main Street, U.S.A. in the Magic Kingdom's utilidor

I hosted a "wrap" party for a multi-week film shoot in the Hollywood Tower of Terror. Nothing quite like pizza in the library at midnight when the building was completely empty. A hauntingly good time was had by all.

My supervisor once threw me a baby shower. I never heard of a guy getting a baby shower, but it was a generous thought, and my wife and children were all invited. It was the first time I ever saw a diaper cake, but those diapers came in handy with the birth of our daughter.

In the preface of this book, Danni Mikler talked about teaming up with Epcot president George Kalogridis to serve chili, sweet rolls, and hot chocolate on New Year's Eve to the Cast in the middle of the night. As I recall, Danni usually served treats and refreshments to Cast Members at the Cast Services building on Christmas Eve most years. It was a selfless way she celebrated her birthday.

What do all these ideas have in common? They are informal ways Cast Members celebrated and reached out to each other. And in many ways, they are often more remembered than the formal events, so make sure that you have a mix of both.

HAVING FUN DOING THE IMPOSSIBLE
LEADERS MAKE THE WORK ITSELF FUN

"It's kind of fun to do the impossible."

Those words from Walt Disney underscore what made working at Disney so wonderful. Walt also noted: **"Most of my life I have done what I wanted to do. I have had fun on the job. I have never been able to confine that fun to office hours."**

Even Michael Eisner and Frank Wells found work fun in their first years. Frank noted: "There's no more fun in this world than this company. Michael and I are still like two little kids. We call each other up and say, 'Listen to this!'"

Many of those quotes resonate with me personally. I love work. I love what I do for work. It's fantastic when someone's work creates amazing results. It's a gift when you can do that in a way that is simply fun and exciting. When that happens, you are probably the luckiest person on earth. In life, 99.99% of most people are in jobs that are hard, difficult, and painful. They are disengaged, or at best, simply checked out. When the opposite happens, it's indeed fortunate.

As a Cast Member at Disney, I was very lucky.

When I think about what personally engaged me as a Cast Member at Disney—where I really had fun—my mind goes back to the days I was assigned to be responsible for the development of the customer service programming. With a master's degree in training & development, I was comfortable with creating curriculum, but delivering instruction on customer service was new to me. I observed it frequently at Disney, but I couldn't define it, much less put it in a framework that would become a multi-day training program.

I was assigned to work with Judi Daley. Judi could be appropriately described as *the* Mary Poppins of Disney Guest service. She had worked at Walt Disney World since its opening, and had been in operational leadership roles throughout the organization. In particular, she had the responsibility for several decades of hosting every VIP (Very Important Person) who visited Walt Disney World. From presidents to kings, from movie stars to rock stars, she hosted them. She knew how to create "Practically Perfect" customer service in every way.

She brought that leadership to our development of the customer service programming at The Disney Institute. She had an insight that was so beyond the surface of simply smiling and being friendly. She understood the processes, systems, products, and services that created a great Guest experience. With that knowledge, she took me under her wing and gave me an education on the subject that you could not get elsewhere. She gave me a new lens for understanding Guests that was truly insightful. I saw the company from perspectives I had never seen in my decades of being a Guest at the parks.

Then, when the programming we created came together, she gave it a finesse of its own. Just getting ready for a 3.5 day workshop was equivalent to creating a Thanksgiving banquet for 35-40 people. She helped us to organize details I would have never paid attention to. We worked for days prior getting everything in order and on the day of the program, we spent hours in advance setting the classroom up to make it as perfect as possible. I would go home exhausted, but invigorated.

She created an arc to our workshops that made the entire program riveting and enjoyable. Around every turn she had some clever insight or surprise for those attending. Little details, like using graphics to express a statement on the white board to catch the participant's attention. For graduation, she orchestrated a show-stopping conclusion with Sarge from Toy Story lining up everyone for certificates.

It was fun! It was engaging. I was proud to be part of something that was so universally accepted by people from corporations and public organizations big and small. I credit Judi as a leader for making that so. She was a strawberry blonde Mary Poppins—in the most delightful way.

Leadership & You

As a leader, consider the following:

- Who creates the fun? Does it always come down from management? When is it something that came up from the ranks that they can take ownership of?

- Is everyone a part of the fun? Does it represent a "clique" of the organization, or is it a place for all?

- Where's management? It's one thing to have an open door policy. It's another to be found in "their territory" having fun with your front line on their terms.

- What does "fun" look like in our organization?

- How do you provide informal, as well as formal, ways to celebrate and engage your employees?

- Is "fun" fun to everyone? How do we meet everyone's sense of "fun"?

- Who holds the keys to having "fun"? Can anyone hold them?

- How do you make working and accomplishing great things fun?

SECTION
IV

PUTTING IT TOGETHER

"I think if there's any part I've played...the vital part is coordinating these talents, and encouraging these talents, and carrying them down a certain line. It's like pulling together a big orchestra. They're all individually very talented. I have an organization who are really specialists. You can't match them anywhere in the world for what they can do. But they all need to be pulled together, and that's my job."

--Walt Disney

17

LEADERSHIP ON PARADE
A CASE STUDY ON LEADERSHIP

We come to a place where we put it all together. We've looked at
it from two important perspectives: Results and Relationships. But
the challenge isn't just about accomplishing goals. It isn't just
about building camaraderie. It's about attaining those results
while working effectively with others. And not just about doing
both—but doing both extremely well. That's the premise of this
chapter—excellence. This chapter provides a case study of a
leader who truly excelled at both results and relationships. It is the
story of Mr. G.

Addressing the Business of Show Business
LEADERS MAKE BOLD MOVES TO ATTAIN RESULTS

People know of *Disney on Ice*, but it's an older generation that
knows of *Disney on Parade*, which was a phenomenal success as an
arena show in the early 1970s. It was more of a pageant rather
than an ice show. Hence, veterans of the show will refer to it as
Disney on Wood. But it was one way Disney was trying to do
something unique in the wake of Walt's passing.

The show was the brainchild of Thomas Sarnoff, youngest son of
Robert Sarnoff, famous as the president of NBC and CEO of
RCA. *The Wonderful World of Disney* was on a major timeslot on
NBC Sunday nights. Thomas Sarnoff saw this as a great way of
bringing the show into cities across America. Disney saw it also as
a great way to promote the brand, and particularly, to introduce

their costumed characters and entertainment to the East Coast in preparation for what would eventually become the Walt Disney World Resort. Sarnoff attracted the attention of Disney, and together, they formed a company known as NAWAL. NA stood for the first two letters in National Broadcasting Company. WAL was the three first letters in Walt Disney Productions. NBC became the general partner; Disney was the limited partner.

Disney was originally responsible for the creative side of the house. NBC was to provide the financial side. Most of the creativity came from Walt Disney Productions and, specifically, Disneyland, which built sets and provided elaborate costumes. The show was originally produced under a man named Bob Jani. He would largely become famous later on for the Main Street Electrical Parade (which drew its ideas from the ball gowns that lit up in the first *Disney on Parade* show) and for other important entertainment contributions. But all of that would come much, much later.

In 1969, after a year of planning, the show was launched, with spending at a stated $2.5 million. Casting calls were put out in the Los Angeles papers. According to Bobby Squires, who was one of the original Cast of the first *Alice* unit, they did an initial cut. Then they invited those auditioning to participate in a six-week process where they did further dance auditions for the show, were introduced to character performing, and were scrutinized. After all, anyone working for Disney had to be fairly clean cut, just like those in the parks. In the end, a final Cast was selected. The show did a trial run in Long Beach, then headed to Chicago for its premiere

Interest in the show was high, but so were the costs. The show ran nearly three hours, included a Cast of nearly 100 performers, and required 40 trucks to get it to Chicago. When it left Chicago, the trucks were cut down in number, but it was still suffering from the weight of its size. Other event shows like Ice Capades and Ringling Brothers Circus already had the best dates. Disney, on the other hand, had a tour lineup that required crossing all over the country in an effort to make it to the next show. Yes, the show was phenomenally popular and well received critically, but its costs were too high. Something had to be done. NBC took the lead. They brought in "Mr. G."

Michael M. Grilikhes or "Mr. G.", as the Cast knew him, was previously a producer for NBC. He had been in theater and entertainment for all of his life and had a variety of experiences. The husband of Laraine Day, a popular movie star of the time, he had a terrific sense of the theatrical and what audiences liked. He was flown over to the show to help work out the problems. The Cast didn't know whom he was at first—just someone walking around with a cane. But Mr. G. took a look at what was happening and made an assessment. He said that within a few weeks they could fix the problems with the show, if they stopped touring. But if they kept touring, it would take longer and they would still bleed money. Disney opted for continuing the tour. Mr. G. changed the show by doing the following:

First off, he reduced the size of the operation, without reducing the quality of the show. Some say that nearly half a million dollars worth of large props were, at some point, thrown out. Also, there was a turntable that was removed from the production. Mr. G. eventually got the show down to 12 trucks and, in some cases, down to eight trucks. He used folks like Steve Ehlers, who created subsequent show units with sets and scenery that were much more collapsible. He got the show down to an operational size that would allow them to travel in a more lean fashion.

Second, he fixed the length and quality of the show. He moved the "Dumbo Circus" section to become part of the finale of the show. He then brought in Tom Hansen to re-choreograph the *Jungle Book* number, which suffered theatrically. Hansen had done a number of TV variety shows, including *Red Skelton* and *Your Hit Parade*. Mr. G. re-recorded sections of the show, insisting that everything recorded be top quality. The show eventually came closer to two hours in length, yet audiences still clamored over the quality of the experience. Later, he brought in top choreographers like Onna White (*The Music Man, Gigi,* and *Mame*), as well as Marc Breaux and Dee Dee Wood (both from *Mary Poppins* and *The Sound of Music*) to work on subsequent shows that would carry the *Disney on Parade* banner.

Third, Mr. G. helped Disney realize that this pageant was more of a dance show, and that dance shows required dancers. Disney was nervous with dancers. Many of those hired had marching band experience, not dance experience. Some were very young, 18-19 years of age, with no experience being on their own, much less working professionally. Divisions were already setting in between those who danced and those who wouldn't be seen with dancers. Something had to be done, and done swiftly.

D-Day came in Charlotte, N.C., not long after Mr. G. stepped in. It was also known as Black Sunday. When the Cast assembled for rehearsal, they soon realized that 15 of their co-performers were not present. Bobby Squires remembers that experience. His roommate, who played Mowgli in the show, was suddenly not there. Mr. G. had acted quickly to remove those performers who simply could not do the show or who were difficult to get along with. He then informed those with great attitudes, but didn't necessarily have the dance skills, that they had to learn the steps quickly, or they wouldn't be allowed to stay on. Mr. G. was decisive, but determined that the show had to stand on a higher plateau if it were to carry the Disney name.

Little by little, more changes were to come, until Disney on Parade became a very successful show. And how successful was it? Well, it probably could never be considered a success in the eyes of management. In fact, Gene Columbus, who managed and led many of the Disney's shows domestically and internationally, noted an occasion when Mr. G. was with Card Walker, president of Walt Disney Productions, talking to an executive about bringing the show back to South Africa. Card began frantically looking everywhere, under papers, in drawers, around the bookshelf. He then interrupted the conversation and excused himself for being distracted. Card said he was still looking for the first dollar he ever made with *Disney on Parade*.

But with that said, the show was still an artistic and popular success. It set records in Madison Square Garden with a record $400,000 in advance sales. It booked 77,255 people in nine days in Salt Lake City. That was some 38 percent of the city's population back then. Critically, the show received rave reviews. It toured in Australia, Asia, Europe, and Latin America. In the end, it is said that it made some $64 million dollars in sales, all under the direction of Mr. G.

According to Beverly Allen, Mr. G.'s assistant: "Mike *was* 'Disney on Parade.' He had a tremendous creative mind. He knew how to grab at the audience's emotions. He was a workaholic. But he was very much a family man."

Mr. G. was capable of running the business of event show management. At one point, there were two shows running in the United States, one in Europe, and one in Australia, while a new one was being produced, ready to go out the following Christmas. In time, there were more than 500 employees all over the world creating these shows. He had a clear vision of creating quality shows—even Broadway-quality shows—at prices that even a family could afford.

Caring for The Cast
LEADERS SHOW THEIR CARE FOR OTHERS

Mr. G. impacted the financial success of the show. But what you do and how you do it are two different matters. What about getting people on board, motivated, and engaged? Being a leader is more than attaining bottom-line results. It's also about relationships. It's about creating a high-performing culture of which those employees can be a part. Let's look at some of the things Mr. G. did that created a group of people who still look back fondly on their time as *Disney on Parade* Cast.

When Mr. G. came on board, it was a time of chaos and change. Not only was the show undergoing considerable change, so too were the lives of the Cast Members. Remember that most of the individuals cast for this show were young people who had not seen much outside of their hometowns, much less had gone "on the road" in a touring show.

Mr. G.'s first job in meeting the needs of the individual Cast Members was to create some sense of normalcy in their lives. Bobby Squires remembers that Mr. G.'s first counsel was to make your life as normal as possible. Even though they were on the road, they needed to do what they normally did when they weren't working. If they went to church back home, then they should go to church on the road. If they liked to go out for Mexican food, they should find a great Mexican restaurant on the road. Mr. G. was a calming influence to those he worked with.

Part of that assurance came as a result of Mr. G.'s patriarchal presence to the show. He became sort of a father figure, noted Beverly Allen. That wasn't difficult in her mind, because that seemed to be what he did at home. He was very much a family man. Whenever his wife Laraine called, he would take the call immediately. He would take some of his kids on the road, to distant ports of call around the world. That same sense of being a dad extended to his work. Even when working from the California office, he would allow Cast Members to contact him personally while they were on the road. Allen would try to play gatekeeper, but the Cast still sought him out with very individual, very personal concerns. In fact, some parents wouldn't let their kid go on the road until they had first talked with Mr. G.

Mr. G., of course, could cut costs when needed, as happened when he first came on board. But he seldom cut costs when it came to the well being of the Cast. For example, the stage flooring was often thrown on top of ice hockey floors, with arena management not wanting to lose the ice. But the ice led to condensation on the floor, which was not good for the dancers. He worked with Coca Cola to figure out some sort of sticky substance that would give the dancers the ability to move about without slipping. Such efforts allowed the Cast to believe in Mr. G. when unions tried to block the success of the show during a union strike in Fort Wayne, Indiana.

Gene Columbus had a great deal of respect for Mr. G., who in turn, gave Columbus tremendous career opportunities. In part, that came through a bonding experience they shared when they first reached New York City. They were meeting in Madison Square Garden's arena offices when they heard a ruckus outside the door. They went outside, only to find the New York United Brotherhood of Electrical Workers upset and cutting their cables. New to the touring scene, Disney had not yet learned the ins and outs of how to deal with unions, and these individuals were upset with Disney's stagehands. Mr. G. and Columbus went to protect the equipment, and Columbus got hit across the face with wire cutters. Mr. G. went to his defense, was kicked in the face, and his jaw was broken. An ambulance took them both away. For months later, the crew saw Mr. G. with his jaw wired together, only able to drink out of a straw.

Events like this led many to follow Mr. G. for years through the shows, even beyond the years of *Disney on Parade*. And Mr. G. was there for his crew as well. Steve Ehlers came during the first show to help make modifications to the original set, creating set designs for remaining shows both nationally and internationally. His talents transformed ordinary arenas into showplaces filled with color and design, all in the truest sense of what Guests would expect from Disney. But later, Ehlers would be completely blinded in an accidental shooting incident in 1973. Undeterred, Mr. G. hired Ehlers anyway to help him design later shows. He simply saw the potential in everyone he met.

Mr. G. would continue leading event shows even after *Disney on Parade* came to a conclusion. He recreated the Broadway show *Peter Pan* starring Cathy Rigby for the arena stage. Then he staged *The Wizard of Oz* as well. Loyal Cast members continued to work with Mr. G. as these shows went on. Afterward, he and his wife continued creating new shows and programming for The Polynesian Cultural Center in Oahu, a work they had begun in the 1960s. Such efforts helped the center to become one of the top tourist destinations in Hawaii, while providing employment to young men and women coming from across Polynesia to attain a college degree.

Mr. G.'s life was about the business and show of show biz. But it was also about the people in that show.

When *Disney on Parade* reached its 25th year anniversary, Mr. G. noted:

> It was one of the most wonderful creative times in my life, where the continuity was there from show to show to reward dedication, discipline, and talent with increased opportunity. The very fact that 25 years after *Disney on Parade* opened, there are still so many to whom that part of their lives has given them a common connection, and common concerns; those whose children are growing up to their parents' memories of a time in their lives that gave them achievement and principles that they still cherish today.

Mr. G. continued to stay very close to members of the Cast through the remaining years. When he passed away in 2007, his daughter Dana was amazed by the number of people who attended his funeral.

All in all, it's how you're remembered long after you've left that ultimately measures you as a leader. Leadership is not just about leading out. It's about leading out on what really matters in life. Jobs and careers ultimately end. But leadership goes on.

18

WE KEEP MOVING FORWARD
LEADERS KEEP MOVING FORWARD

You Can Be a Leader

Let's summarize. Our focus has been around achieving results by effectively working with others. It's been about results and relationships. Here are the key messages:

Leaders attend to results by:	Leaders fortify relationships by:
• Exhibiting a "can do" attitude • Staying the vision • Working hard • Optimizing time • Being resourceful • Learning from their mistakes • Seeking excellence	• Building morale • Establishing trust & empowering others • Flattening the organization • Getting everybody on board • Keeping the sandbox friendly • Communicating • Recognizing others • Making work fun

There are three important messages from this list:

First: These are the practical, very real things leaders can do to be effective. You can get results by practicing the behaviors listed. You can effectively work with others by embodying the practices noted. It's about attaining results by effectively working with others.

Second: These are not things that can only be done by a company like Disney. You can't say "well, a company like Disney can do this, but not a small company like mine." Look at the behaviors noted above. None of these require a big budget. In fact, what is telling about these behaviors is that they are really low/no cost activities that anyone can take on.

Third: They are not behaviors that can only be attended to by an appointed manager. There is nothing that can only be played out by the "guy at the top". Yes, managers should demonstrate these behaviors. But so should any individual in the organization. These are personal behaviors we can all master.

It isn't just Disney. It isn't just managers. It's you.

You.

We Go On

So where do we go from here?

Walt Disney stated: "Around here, however, we don't look backwards for very long. We keep moving forward, opening up new doors and doing new things, because we are curious…and curiosity keeps leading us down new paths."

How does one keep moving forward? The setting of Epcot is a great place to conclude this treatise on leadership. Here we provide two stories. The first includes these lyrics:

We Go On
Every evening
Brings an ending
Every day becomes a legacy
Every sunset
Leads to morning
With the promise of opportunity

These lyrics frame the final moments of *IllumiNations: Reflections of Earth*. How they came to be written by a man who was known for designing fireworks—not writing lyrics—is the story of Don Dorsey.

As an audio producer for parades like the *Main Street Electrical Parade* and *America on Parade*, and a designer/director of fireworks and nighttime spectaculars like *Sorcery in the Sky*, Don Dorsey was tasked with being the creative director when it originally opened as *IllumiNations 2000: Reflections of Earth*.

Don had initially sought out Hans Zimmer, who had composed the soundtrack for *The Lion King*, to work on the show. When Hans realized that he really wasn't available to do the project, he suggested Gavin Greenaway, a talented composer and conductor himself, to write the music. Gavin created, in practically the first take, the music that you hear throughout the performance. But he didn't feel comfortable doing the lyrics, and after seeking the help of others, still could not make it work. Gavin suggested Don try it.

In the midst of this activity, Don Dorsey found out that Mark Nichols, the original director of the project and a friend of Don's, was taken off the project and moved laterally in the organization. Don was heading back to California, and while on a layover in Dallas, called Mark to vent his frustration. Toward the end of the conversation, after both had expressed their disappointment, Don said, "Well...we go on." Later, back on the plane and pondering the words of that conversation, he realized that the message for Epcot's Millennium was really about moving forward. We go on. Don described it as follows:

> Then I thought, that really speaks in a generic way to what has enabled humans to survive. In any day there's up moments, there's down moments and yet the core message of the human race is, "No matter what... we go on."

Or, as Walt Disney stated, "We keep moving forward."

The rest is history, with *IllumiNations: Reflections of Earth* successfully playing for some two decades.

Leadership on Spaceship Earth

The idea that "we go on" has been going on, well, for many a century. And our final story begins a century ago. Years ago, a very smart young man once held the potential of being one of the greatest inventors of the twentieth century. He was accepted—and rejected—by Harvard twice for being too eccentric in his thinking. He was also quite the partier. Something of a "wild lad" on the side, he failed his wife and children, and was a heavy drinker. His daughter Alexandra was very sick at the age of 6 with polio and spinal meningitis. The story is told that one day, wanting to go to a football game, he promised his daughter he would be home later to bring back a souvenir from the game, and to celebrate her birthday.

Three days later, he finally returned home from a long drunken stupor. When he arrived, his wife told him not to waste time apologizing to her, but to go and see his daughter directly. The girl had taken a turn for the worse. The man picked up his daughter. She asked her dad if he had brought the souvenir. In his drunken stupor, he had forgotten. The disappointment on her face was what he saw as she closed her eyes for the last time and died in her father's arms a few hours later.

Depression followed. He resigned from the Navy, where he had formerly been successful. He was out of work over a number of years. In time, the man considered suicide, and he made the decision that would end his life. But then he heard a voice, and that voice said:

"You do not have the right to eliminate yourself. You do not belong to you. You belong to the Universe."

That was the pivot on which, he claimed, his life turned. The one-time loser entered a period of such deep reflection that he was struck silent, then emerged bursting with creativity as he developed technologies that he promised would transform housing, transportation, and urban design.

He would describe that turn around as follows:

> Something hit me very hard once, thinking about what one little man could do. Think of the Queen Mary — the whole ship goes by and then comes the rudder. And there's a tiny thing at the edge of the rudder called a trim tab.

> It's a miniature rudder. Just moving the little trim tab builds a low pressure that pulls the rudder around. Takes almost no effort at all. So I said that the little individual can be a trim tab. Society thinks it's going right by you, that it's left you altogether. But if you're doing dynamic things mentally, the fact is that you can just put your foot out like that and the whole big ship is going to go...

> "If ever someone wanted to write my epitaph, I would want it to say, "'Call me Trim Tab.'"

Some 28 books and 47 honorary degrees later, the man succeeded as a theorist, architect, engineer, designer, inventor, and futurist. You know him as the man who conceived the geodesic sphere known as Spaceship Earth. But the one label he prefers is found next to his name on his gravestone:

> *R. Buckminster Fuller*
> *"Call me Trimtab"*

This is what the man many called "Bucky" once stated:

> When I thought about steering the course of the 'Spaceship Earth' and all of humanity, I saw most people trying to turn the boat by pushing the bow around.

> I saw that by being all the way at the tail of the ship, by just

kicking my foot to one side or the other, I could create the 'low pressure' which would turn the whole ship.

When you walk by that big silver ball at the end of your day at Epcot, know that the man who not only conceived the architectural form of this geodesic masterpiece--but had named it Spaceship Earth--learned during his life what he came here to do.

And so it must be for all of us. Regardless of our position, our title or status, we must learn what we came here to do. And then we must do it. And keep on doing it! That's what Disney does. That's what leaders do. And that's what you should do.

As the song ends:

Moving on
Through the good times and the tears
Ever on
Another thousand circles 'round the sun
A new life has begun
When two of us are one
And we live to keep the promise
We'll go on
Ever on
We'll go on

WHAT STEPS WILL YOU TAKE AS A LEADER?

Individuals just like you are trying to figure out how to not only lead, but also how to create an organization of leadership excellence. J. Jeff Kober has worked with a wide variety of organizations in the private, public and non-profit sectors to help them grow and develop to the next level. From leadership excellence, to improving employee engagement; from creating highly satisfied customers to developing long-term customer loyalty, we have solutions that will set your Chain Reaction of Excellence in motion.

LEADERSHIP EXCELLENCE — HIGHLY ENGAGED EMPLOYEES — HIGHLY SATISFIED CUSTOMERS — LOYALTY & LONG-TERM SUCCESS

Need a keynote speaker? Interested in a workshop or seminar? How about a unique online set of tools you and your employees can use every day? Jeff provides not only these offerings but consulting, organizational development, instructional design, and so much more. He gets into the trench with organizations and helps leaders like you take teams to the next level.

From hospitals to government agencies; from banks to hotels; from associations to universities, Jeff has labored for some thirty-five years to help organizations make real improvements. And he can help you do the same. Just call to discuss your needs and circumstances. He can offer a solution tailored to your unique needs. You can contact Jeff at 407-973-3219, or at jeffkober@gmail.com

Index

Bibliography

Buckminster Fuller's Universe: His Life and Work, by L. Steven Sieden. New York: Basic Books, 2000.

Building a Company: Roy O. Disney and the Creation of an Entertainment Empire, by Bob Thomas. New York: Hyperion, 1998.

Creativity, Inc.: Overcoming the Unseen Forces That Stand in the Way of True Inspiration, by Ed Catmull & Amy Wallace. New York: Random House, 2014.

Designing Disney: Imagineering and the Art of the Show, by John Hench. New York: Disney Editions, 2009.

Disney Magic: The Launching of a Dream, by John Hemingway. New York: Disney Editions Deluxe, 2006.

Disney War, by James B. Stewart. New York: Simon & Schuster, 2006

Disney's Hollywood Studios: From Show Biz to Your Biz, by J. Jeff Kober. Theme Park Press, 2014.

Dream It! Do It!: My Half-Century Creating Disney's Magic Kingdoms, by Marty Sklar. New York: Disney Editions Deluxe, 2013.

House of Leaves, by Mark Z. Danielewski. New York: Pantheon, 2000.

Ink & Paint: The Women of Walt Disney's Animation, by Mindy Johnson. New York: Disney Editions, 2017

It's Kind of a Cute Story, by Rolly Crump and Jeff Heimbuch. Baltimore, Maryland: Bamboo Forest Publishing, 2012

Quotable Walt Disney, by Disney Book Group. New York: Disney Editions Deluxe, 2001

Lead with Your Customer: Transform Culture and Brand into World-Class Excellence, by Mark David Jones and J. Jeff Kober, Washington D.C.: ATD Press, 2010

One Little Spark!: Mickey's Ten Commandments and The Road to Imagineering, by Marty Sklar. New York: Disney Editions, 2015.

Prince of the Magic Kingdom: Michael Eisner and the Re-Making of Disney, by Joe Flower. Hoboken, NJ: Wiley, 1991

Realityland: True-Life Adventures at Walt Disney World, by David Koenig. Irvine, California: Bonaventure Press, 2007

Roller Coasters, Flumes and Flying Saucers: The Story of Ed Morgan and Karl Bacon, Ride Inventors of the Modern Amusement Park, by Robert R. Reynolds. Bend Oregon: Northern Lights Publishing, 1999.

Spinning Disney's World: Memories of a Magic Kingdom Press Agent, by Charles Ridgway. New York: The Intrepid Traveler, 2007.

To Infinity and Beyond!: The Story of Pixar Animation Studios, by Karen Paik. San Francisco: Chronicle Books, 2007.

The 7 Habits of Highly Effective People: Powerful Lessons in Personal Change, by Stephen R. Covey. New York: Free Press, 1989.

The Creative Compass: Writing Your Way from Inspiration to Publication, by Dan Millman & Sierra Prasada. Novato, California: HJ Kramer New World Library, 2013.

The Forty Rules of Love: A Novel of Rumi, by Elif Shafak. New York: Viking, 2010.

The Haunted Mansion: From the Magic Kingdom to the Movies, by Jason Surrell. New York: Disney Editions, 2009

The Illusion of Life—Disney Animation, by Frank Thomas and Ollie Johnston. New York: Disney Editions, 1981.

The Marauders, by Charlton Ogburn. New York: Harper, 1959.

The Pixar Touch: The Making of a Company, by David A. Price. New York: Vintage, 2009.

The Story of Philosophy: The Lives and Opinions of the World's Greatest Philosophers, by Will Durant. New York: Pocket Books, 1991.

The Wonderful World of Customer Service at Disney. by J. Jeff Kober. Kissimmee, Florida: Performance Journeys Publishing; 2013.

Walt Disney: An American Original, by Bob Thomas. New York: Simon and Schuster, 1976.

Walt Disney: The Triumph of the American Imagination, by Neal Gabler. New York: Alfred A. Knopf, 2006.

Walt Disney's Imagineering Legends and the Genesis of the Disney Theme Park, by Jeff Kurtti. New York: Disney Editions, 2007.

Window on Main Street: 35 Years of Creating Happiness at Disneyland Park, by Van Arsdale France. Laughter Publications, Stabur Press, 1991.

Work in Progress, by Michael Eisner. New York: Random House, 1998

Magazine & Newspaper Articles

"Bob Iger: Disney's fun king," by Jennifer Reingold. Fortune Magazine, May 9, 2012.

"Bob Iger, James Cameron Open Pandora: World of Avatar at Walt Disney World," by Lawrence Yee. Variety, May 24, 2017.

"Bob Iger Showman of the Year: Striving for Perfection," by James Rainey. Variety, November 22, 2016.

"How Bob Iger works," by Devin Leonard, Fortune, December 6, 2007

"Innovation lessons from Pixar: An interview with Oscar-winning director Brad Bird," by Hayagreeva Rao, Robert Sutton, and Allen P. Webb. McKingsey Quarterly, April 2008.

"It's a Small World," by Mara Hvistendahl. Delta Sky Magazine, September 2016.

"Man who sank the Mark Twain," by Carma Wadley. Deseret News, October 21, 2005. "The father of Guestology: An interview with Bruce Laval," by Robert C. Ford and Duncan Dickson. The Journal of Applied Management & Entrepreneurship, January 2009.

"The Secrets of Great Groups" by Warren Bennis. *Leader to Leader*, Winter 1997.

"Who's the Mystery Man in Epcot's Garage? Neither Woz nor Jobs," by Andy Denhart. Wired, January 31, 2008

Blogs & Websites

"Aulani Essay," by Martin Charlot.
http://www.martincharlot.com/aulani-essay.htm

"Disney at Work: Neal McCord," by J. Jeff Kober. MousePlanet, August 6, 2009.
www.mouseplanet.com

"Engineering the EPCOT Center Dream: Imagineer Art Frohwerk and Department 510," By J. Jeff Kober. MousePlanet, September 27, 2007.

"Interview: Don Dorsey—IllumiNations: Reflections of Earth (transcription)," by Scott Wolf. Mouse Clubhouse Blog, January 25, 2009.
http://shaniwolf.com/interview-don-dorsey-illuminations-reflections-of-earth-transcription/

"Leading Disney on Parade: Part I," by J. Jeff Kober. MousePlanet, January 22, 2009.

"Leading Disney on Parade: Part II," by J. Jeff Kober. MousePlanet, February 5, 2009.

"Renie Bardeau: The Man Who Shot Walt Disney," by Jim Korkis. MousePlanet, March 14, 2012.
www.mouseplanet.com

"Tokyo DisneySea Project," OLC Group
http://www.olc.co.jp/en/company/history/history05.html

"Twelve Stories of Disneyland: Part Two," by Jim Korkis. MousePlanet, December 21, 2016.
www.mouseplanet.com

DVDs & Podcasts

The Boys: The Sherman Brothers' Story, by Walt Disney Studios Motion Pictures, directed by Jeffrey C. Sherman and Gregory V. Sherman.

The Joe Rohde Interviews / The Season Pass /
www.seasonpasspodcast.com

The Tom Morris Interview with Tony Baxter! / The Season Pass /
www.seasonpasspodcast.com

The Tony Baxter Inteview Part 1! / The Season Pass /
www.seasonpasspodcast.com

Tim Delaney Interview part 2 / The Season Pass /
www.seasonpasspodcast.com

Preserved Presentation: 2 with Merrit, Lynxwiler, R. Crump, C. Crump, Sotto, Davisson and More!/ The Season Pass / **www.seasonpasspodcast.com**

The Mark Eades Interview / The Season Pass /
www.seasonpasspodcast.com

MORE EXCELLENCE!

WANT MORE FOR YOUR ORGANIZATION? J. JEFF KOBER OFFERS THE FOLLOWING SOLUTIONS FOR TAKING YOUR WORKPLACE TO NEW LEVELS OF EXCELLENCE!

PERFORMANCE JOURNEYS

DISNEY AT WORK

WORLD CLASS BENCHMARKING

Real, practical and proven ideas for improving leadership, employee engagement, the customer experience and more! Our thought leadership offers you insights that will take your organization to the next level!

Best in business ideas from the "Happiest Place on Earth"! Look to Jeff to offer keynotes, seminars, books and more about great ideas from Disney! Better yet, come visit the parks with him and experience the business behind the magic!

Founded by Jeff and former Disney leader Mark David Jones, World Class Benchmarking highlights not only great benchmarking ideas & models from Disney, but also best-of-the-best practices from other great organizations!

PERFORMANCEJOURNEYS.COM

DISNEYATWORK.COM

WORLDCLASSBENCHMARKING.COM

WANT TO BRING GREAT IDEAS BACK TO YOUR WORKPLACE?

Beyond the consulting, books, and workshops, try our new online learning that bring great tools and ideas from many organizations—including Disney—to your workplace! It's our *Excellence and You* series. Visit any of the above websites to learn more! Or just call J. Jeff Kober at 407-973-3219 or JeffKober@gmail.com.

n/pod-product-compliance

1B/1962

0 9 9 9 1 7 2 6 0 5 *